The Grass is Greener Where Its Watered

All A's for Successful Relationships

To

Shan

Best wishes

Dr. Charles Kra

**From the Vatican
to the Playboy Mansion**

The Grass
is Greener
Where it's
Watered

All A's for a Successful Relationship
Father Charles D. Ara

The Grass is Greener Where It's Watered

Learn love's secrets from the priest who married Hugh Hefner to Kimbe Conrad at the Playboy Mansion in 1989. Drawing on his 36 years of working w couples as both priest and marital therapist, Charles Ara tells how to make a lc relationship work. In a sometimes humorous and witty fashion, the author sugge ways to get an A in love. Subtitled *All As' for a Successful Relationship*, the rea will discover new ways to practice appreciation, attention, affection, acceptan and other A's. Affirmations and practical suggestions follow each chapter. A m for any couple wanting to make and/or keep their marriage, in the words of song, "ageless and evergreen."

To have Charles Ara present a workshop, speak to your group, perform a weddi ceremony, for personal counseling sessions, or to order additional copies, pleas call or write to: EJ Publishing, 11215 Park Street, Cerritos, CA 90703, by phone: (562) 865-4075

First published in 1992 in North America by EJ Publishing, 11215 Park Street, Cerritos, CA 90703, U.S.A. (562) 865-4075

© 1992 by EJ Publishing

Library of Congress Number 91-76172

ISBN 0-9630928-0-4

Cover Layout: Martin Ara

Printed and bound in the United States of America.

Dedication

"You give but little when you give of your possessions: it is when you give of yourself that you truly give."

With these words of the Lebanese poet, Kahlil Gibran, I dedicate this book to my father, Daniel Saleem Ara (1903-1982) who:

1) loved my mother, Margaret, for over 50 years

2) saw good in every human being who came his way

3) was the all time giver of warmth

4) taught me to accept every human being I met

5) showed me how to water the grass

I also dedicate this book to Shirley, my lover, my teacher and best friend who has stood by me and watered our relationship for over 21 years.

Finally, I dedicate this book to our five children

Martin John
Jose Anthony
Rana   Annette
Dawna Gibrana
Matthew Charles

with the hope that they and their future partners practice the A's of successful relationships.

Acknowledgements

I'd like to thank a few folks who've supported and advised me, offered suggestions, read the manuscript, or just plain been helpful during the writing of this book: Anne Copeland MacCallum, who assisted with production. Writers who assisted, John Trausch and Anne Marie Bustamente, advisers Margret McBride and Winifred Golden, my college students who helped with the lists on how to get time alone together, things that could help or damage relationships, couples from my parishes who contributed their stories, couples from therapy who allowed their story to be told, my family and many supportive relatives.

The inside art is by Alberta Milton, the one drawing in the Introduction is by Christopher Schlarb, and the cover photo is by Michael O'Brien, Sr.

Contents

From the Vatican to the Playboy Mansion: The Journey of Love

When love calls to you, follow
 And when its wings enfold you, yield
 And when love speaks to you, believe
 And think not that you can direct the course of love,
For love, if it finds you worthy, directs your course
-- Kahlil Gibran

From the Vatican to the Playboy Mansion, and many places in between, the course of love has led me to many fascinating experiences. My own journey of love began with my parent's love for each other which brought me into the world. Early in life, love called me to a relationship with God, the priesthood and the Church. Love then directed me to Shirley, my wife and best friend. Love has brought me five wonderful children.

I have said Mass in St. Peter's Cathedral in the Vatican, over the tomb of St. Francis in Assisi, in the Catacombs of Rome, in St. Patrick's Cathedral in New York and on July 1, 1989 I performed Hugh Hefner's wedding to Kimberley Conrad at the wishing well of the Playboy Mansion.

As a Roman Catholic parish priest, single and celibate for 15 years, and now, as a married priest and licensed marital therapist for the past 21 years, I have been intimately involved with married couples.

In a sense, I am in a unique position to have studied marriages from both the viewpoint of a celibate and a married man. Many of my hours as a parish priest were spent counseling couples preparing for marriage or counseling couples with their problems after they were married. Most of my working hours now as a therapist are spent with couples helping them to solve their conflicts and improve their marriages.

My many years of experience with couples have given me some valuable insights on why some marriages work and why some do not. These insights form the basis of this book. The inspiration to write this book came to me the day after I performed the Hefner wedding at the Playboy Mansion.

It was a gorgeous July afternoon, sunny and warm, and so clear the air sparkled. Baroque horns and violins charmed the arriving wedding guests, seeming to draw them to the chairs arranged in neat rows on the grassy floor of an enchanted outdoor cathedral with the endless sky as our ceiling and a wishing well as our altar. It was a lovely spot for a wedding, surrounded by trees and flowers and the Georgian, stone-walled elegance of the Playboy mansion.

Of all the weddings I have performed, the marriage of Hugh Hefner and Kimberley Conrad is the one people want to know about. After the publicity given to that marriage ceremony in the world wide media, I became somewhat of an instant celebrity as the maverick priest who conducted the rites.

I was invited to appear on several television and radio talk shows to discuss the wedding. The two most frequently asked questions were, "Do you think the Hefner marriage will last?" and "Is that playboy going to stay with one woman?"

I answer "Yes, if Hef and Kimberley 'water the grass,'" a phrase I use during many wedding ceremonies, including theirs. I ask couples "How should you care for your love?" Then I answer for them: "Very carefully. You have to remember that the grass isn't greener on the other side, the grass is greener where it is watered." So I told Hef and Kimberley, "Water the grass!!!" I then gave them, as I give to all my couples, four of my A's of watering a love relationship. The A's I gave Hef & Kim were appreciation, attention, affection and acceptance.

The title of this book *The Grass is Greener Where it is Watered* came to me as people kept asking me the same questions over and over again about the Hefner marriage. I believe they ask because they secretly wonder if any marriage or relationship will last. Is it simply a matter of luck, or is there something a couple can do to ensure their relationship will not only endure, but will be successful, meaningful, growth oriented, and happy? This book came about as an answer to those questions.

Traditionally we throw rice on newly married couples, wish them luck, and give them a casserole dish or a cake server. Privately we cross our fingers because we know the odds; we know how fragile relationships are, and how easily they fall apart. And from our own experiences in life, we wish we had something that would be more useful in life than a cake server.

Though the prospects might seem somewhat dismal, I believe that we are not helpless, and that we can, in fact, make successful relationships if we are willing to work on them. The key is to recognize that "the grass is greener where it's watered."

During thirty-six years of working with, counseling, and observing married couples as a priest, and then as a counselor, I have discovered that successful marriages or other forms of relationships seemed to practice certain principles, principles I call the A's of successful relationships. As you read through the book, each A will be explained and illustrated. At the end of each chapter, you will find quizzes and checklists to help you determine where you are now and to begin to create a new road map of progress.

In the book, I draw an analogy between gardening and relationships. In gardening, water and sunlight, good soil, essential nutrients, and weed and pest eradication are essential. Of course, awareness of these important factors alone will not create a healthy garden; you must be willing to work at it constantly.

Most people understand the necessity of watering a lawn. They know that without water the grass will wither and die. What many people don't realize is that relationships need to be cared for in much the same way we care for the lawn. But how do you water a relationship? What do you use for water? The answer is something I have designated "all A's for a successful relationship."

The A'S of Successful Relationships are Easy

Couples come to me because they want to know how to make their relationships work. Some of them are in the premarital stage, others are on the verge of divorce or breakup, and the rest are at every stage between. Whatever the state of their relationships are, they always seem surprised to learn that, as with anything valuable in life, their relationships are lost because they are not properly cared for.

Relationships are like gardens, I tell them, and like gardens, they must be cared for. How do you care for your love? VERY CAREFULLY, because even the least amount of neglect can create weeds and pests that destroy the very soil of the relationship. For those who are not into gardening, you can surely relate to the fact that it doesn't take a sledgehammer to destroy a car. Just don't ever get it serviced. Neglect will destroy a car, a garden, and most definitely, it will destroy a relationship.

4

The good news is that caring for a relationship is easy, even for those of you who claim to have a brown thumb. It doesn't require long hours or strenuous labor to maintain a well-kept garden; a few minutes a day is all it takes to water and inspect for weeds and pests. You might spend a couple of hours every week for jobs such as fertilizing and planting, but once the garden is in good shape, it takes very little time to keep it up on a daily basis. The same is true for your relationship. It takes only a few minutes a day, a couple of hours once or twice a week, and a few weekends throughout the year to make it work. How many of you spend more time on your yards than you do on your relationship?

The A's of Successful
Relationships are Simple

In working with couples, I find that many people believe love relationships are complicated and mysterious. How can you understand love, they ask. Isn't love based on chemistry? Isn't it mystical and magical, popping up out of nowhere and disappearing just as suddenly? Isn't that what happens in the movies? Two people meet, take one good look at each other, and WHAM, it's love at first sight.

Back in my days as a parish priest, I remember Cathy, an attractive 17-year-old who had been a part of our church youth group, bringing Peter into my church office on a Monday evening to talk about getting married. They held hands and sat close together.

"Father," said Cathy, "Peter and I would like you to marry us next Saturday."

"Oh my goodness," I said, "How long have you known each other?" Without batting an eye she looked starry-eyed at Peter and replied, "37 days."

I knew this couple was not ready for life after cutting the wedding cake. They hardly knew each other. Were they taking marriage seriously, or were they just in heat?

Fortunately, it was church policy to delay a wedding until a three-month preparation had taken place.

In truth, we all know there is no such thing as love at first sight. In fact, love never just happens. In real life, people meet each other, and they may like what they see. Then they begin the process of getting to know one another and to feel emotions for one another. It takes some time before they get over the newness and the "looking good" stage to seeing each other as each person actually is. It is during that stage that people either grow to love each other or their relationships fall apart.

But what really causes love to grow? It may seem magical, but in reality it's seeing your partner as he or she really is, and

6

appreciating those qualities fully. How do we do this? What are the things a couple can do to cause love to mature and grow? As I have stated before, it can all happen with the A's for a successful relationship.

The A's for a successful relationship are like an alphabet for a successful life. They are: Attention, Appreciation, Affection, Appeal, Animation, Acceptance, Adaptability, Affirmation, Affability, Allowance, Awareness, Amiability, Assertiveness, and Abidance. Everything necessary to plant and grow a successful relationship is contained in these "A's," but they are not complicated or mysterious. They are as simple as hugging and listening. They are as simple as caring. Do you care about your relationship? Do you care enough to invest measurable effort for immeasurable returns?

The A's of Successful Relationships are Timeless

Not only are the A's of successful relationships easy and uncomplicated, they are also proven over time. Not one item is a buzz word or an exotic technical technique. The A's have existed as long as relationships have existed. How long is that? I'm not certain, but one thing I am sure of: as long as there have been people, there has been the need for affection, appreciation, acceptance, and the rest of the A's because they are basic human needs we all share. This book offers you a legacy of wisdom that is well-worn, tear-stained, and priceless, wisdom that has passed down through many generations.

My years of experience with couples have given me insight on why some relationships work while others do not. Insights are perfect little gems of knowledge that illuminate and enable the human mind to comprehend underlying truths, to see below the surface where lie all our reasons for doing the things we do. Insights are priceless. They can change your life. The express purpose of this book is to empower you with these insights because I am committed to helping couples to succeed in their relationships. That is my purpose, and probably yours as well if you are reading this book.

We have always had these needs and emotions that we don't understand. The difference is that as the 21st century approaches, the human race, as a whole, possesses not only the capacity to understand emotions and feelings, but the ability to communicate that understanding to a degree that is historically unmatched. We are provided with the tools for self-improvement through mass distribution of literature, through radio and television, through adult education classes, and through the many self-help groups. Understanding is a commodity available to everyone. As people have become better educated about human relations, there is also an unprecedented willingness and desire to experience relationships to the fullest.

The A's of Successful Relationships are Fun

Easy, simple, and timeless. Is that enough? Are you willing to put time and effort into your relationship just because it's easy, simple, and timeless? I would venture to say not, because these things might also be boring and empty. But if it promised fun, wouldn't that make a difference? Don't people get married because they want to enjoy life, to feel good about themselves, and to have fun?

When a couple comes to me to arrange a wedding, I always ask them to name some endearing qualities about each other. Over and over again, they list such qualities as "He listens to me," "She makes me feel good about myself," "He's a real friend," and "She makes me laugh and cry." People get married because they feel good when they're together. People get married because they make each other feel good.

Never Stop Courting Your Mate

How is it, then, that so many couples seem to excel at making each other feel bad? Before they get together they are high on positive emotions. They like everything about each other, and each believes the other is perfect. Do you believe it is an exaggeration? You'd be surprised to hear how often people tell me, "He's perfect, Dr. Ara," and "She's an angel." The truth is, no one is perfect, and no one is an angel. Sooner or later, usually shortly after the wedding ceremony, the truth comes out. The emotional high begins to subside, the glow of perfection slowly diminishes, and before you know it, a couple goes from being friends and lovers to being husband and wife. Talk about a drag. Many couples go on like that for years, especially people who don't like excitement. But the closeness and the fun of their courting days are gone forever.

Never stop courting your mate. If you have stopped, you need to begin again. Remember that when you're courting, your emotions effect your behavior, but when you are married or involved in a relationship, your behavior effects your emotions. Water your love relationship every day. Practice the A's every day, and you will never stop having fun.

ON THE SAME TEAM

The A's of Successful Relationships are for You

If you already have a happy relationship, undoubtedly you are practicing some of the A's, but there is always the risk that you might stop practicing them is you are not aware of what you are doing to make it all work. Reading this book will show you what you are doing right, and at the same time bring to light the weak areas of your relationship. For those of you with good relationships, this book is a preventive maintenance manual. However, if your relationship is less than perfect, or in real trouble, this book will be a repair manual.

FRIENDS & LOVERS

HUSBAND & WIFE

I have seen couples without hope build brand new relationships, and I have seen couples with a total breakdown in communication learn to talk to each other again, and learn to trust each other once more. It's not magic. It's not a quick fix. It requires reasonable effort, but for those who are willing, this book will supply the water.

The remaining chapters of this book will explain and illustrate, one at a time, the A's for successful relationships. At the end of the chapters are quizzes, checklists and suggestions to help you determine where you are now in your relationship, and to help take you where you would like to go with it.

Travel through the book at your own pace. You may wish to take one A each day, one a week, or one a month. Taking one A at a time and practicing it for one or two weeks before adding another one, often works best.

The A's are so important that I recite them at every wedding I perform, and I guarantee that if a couple faithfully practices the essential A's, their marriage will not only succeed, it will be a genuine adventure.

Both Hands Must Clap To Make Noise

Just as it takes two hands to clap, so it takes both partners in the relationship to practice the A's to make the marriage work.

Getting A's in your relationship can be habit-forming once you get started. Just relax, enjoy the journey. You will find that once set in motion, your new behavior will make its own path.

It is my hope and prayer that the following chapters will provide you with the inspiration to make your relationship a little better for having crossed my path, the path of a married Roman Catholic priest.

PRAYING FOR A GOOD
CATHOLIC MAN

Chapter 1

Friends and Lovers Forever: Attention

How Time is slipping underneath our Feet:
Unborn To-morrow, and dead Yesterday,
Why fret them if today be sweet.
                    --Edward Fitzgerald

When couples are courting, they move heaven and earth to find time to be together, yet once they've married or have been together for a while, they often lose each other amid the business of earning a living, raising a family, running kids to day-care, and the many other things that get in the way.

The Priest and the Parishioner

Let me tell you a story about a middle-aged Roman Catholic priest who fell in love with one of his parishioners.

Each night Shirley prayed to the Lord to send her a good Catholic man to marry. Apparently the Lord heard her prayer and decided that Father Charlie was the man for the job. Parish priests are very busy men, and Father Charlie was no exception. His duties began early each day with morning mass, and ended late in the evenings with bible study or night prayers. And Shirley was a very busy young woman, working as a teacher coordinator in the parish, and actively involved in civil rights and fair housing.

Clearly, there was little opportunity for them to spend time together. And lack of time was not their only obstacle. You don't have to be Catholic to know the Church does not encourage priests to fall in love, let alone to get married. Married priests were not then, and are still not, recognized by the Church hierarchy.

Despite all the obstacles, these two people managed to fall in love, and somehow, every day, they discovered ways to be with each. You might even say they moved heaven and earth to be together. And this is the moral of the story. Love is so precious and powerful that men and women will sacrifice just about anything to have it. You all know about the King who gave up his crown for love, and Father Charlie, along with many others, gave up his parish, and his job for a lifetime to marry the woman he loved.

86,400 Seconds

For those still not convinced they can find the time for their mate, I say, "I have twenty-four hours in my day. How many hours do you have in your day?" Unless they're trying to be funny, they usually answer, "Twenty-four."

"Ah," I say, "twenty-four. You have twenty-four hours in your day, and so do I."

Then I ask them, "Do you know how many seconds there are in twenty-four hours?" Of course they don't. "86,400!" I tell them. "86,400 seconds in every day. That's a lot of seconds."

Sometimes I get THAT look when I say that. You know, the look that says, that's a lot of seconds. So what? So I tell them, "The problem isn't that we don't have enough time. The problem is what we do with the time we do have."

At this point, some people get a big smile on their faces, indicating that a light has just turned on in their heads. It's that light that goes on when we see something in a way we've never seen it before. Others begin to get a little annoyed, thinking that I am trying to impress them with my arithmetic, or that perhaps I'm oversimplifying the problem. Sometimes it's really hard to convince people it's that simple. But it is. We all have the same number of hours and seconds in every day, and we choose how to use them. We are in control. We make the decisions.

Right now, you can choose to spend X amount of seconds, minutes, or hours a day with your mate. Start out small. Set aside fifteen seconds a day to look into each other's eyes, and to renew your commitment to neglect the whole world rather than each other. Once you make that decision, make it the number one priority of your day. Neglect the whole world, neglect your job, and your hobbies before you neglect those fifteen seconds with the most important person in your life.

Every day, look into the eyes of your mate, your lover, your friend. It only takes a moment, and it doesn't cost a lot of money. Do this to remind yourself to neglect the whole world rather than each other.

It's important to take time to make meaningful eye contact with your mate daily. Once is imperative, but more is better in this case.

Every Motel in the State

One of the great things about my job is all the interesting people I get to meet and talk with. I always learn something from these encounters, and, sometimes, the lesson is so profound, that it becomes a story I tell over and over again. Like the story of Dottie and Sy.

Dottie and Sy were married twenty-eight years, when suddenly, Sy died. About a month after Sy's death, I went to see Dottie, and to offer condolences. I had known the two of them for a long time. As I drove to their house, I tried to formulate what words, if any, I might say to offer this tragedy-stricken woman some small measure of comfort and encouragement. I tried to prepare myself for what was sure to be a very sad and emotionally taxing visit.

Imagine my surprise when I arrived to find, not a broken and disheartened widow, but a calm and peaceful woman who didn't look like she just lost her husband. At first, I didn't know what to think. But in a few minutes, I began to see the reason for her peaceful acceptance of the situation.

"Sy and I had a wonderful marriage," Dottie told me. "He was such a good husband. I thank God for giving me a husband like that." Then she went on to say something that really knocked my socks off, "You know, Sy and I knew every motel in the state of California."

"What do you mean, Dottie?" I said, quietly thinking that some people certainly are different in real life than they seem when I talk with them.

Dottie then told me how every month for twenty-eight years, she and Sy went to a different motel for two nights and three days. One whole weekend out of every month! They devoted that time to each other. They spent that money on each other. They never made excuses to each other; they simply did it. They knew the secret that so many couples desperately need to know, that money spent on each other is money well spent.

Time spent with each other is always time well spent. Dottie and Sy never let anything or anyone come before their devotion to each other. And that devotion brought them so much pleasure, and stored up so many good memories, that Dottie had the best consolation of all when Sy was no longer around to share with her. The knowledge that they had lived and loved to the fullest all the days of their marriage is wonderfully comforting.

Go Ye Therefore and Watch the Dancing Waters

By contrast, I recall a couple who came to see me not too long ago. The couple, Rick and Diane, were one of the angriest couples I've ever seen. They were so angry that they couldn't even talk to each other. They sat in my office hurtling accusations like arrows at each other, each one unable to say even one nice thing about the other. Generally even couples who are getting a divorce are able to think of one nice thing about the other person. Rick and Diane were each certain that they had married the earthly incarnation of evil. Something had to be done to relieve the pressure before somebody got killed.

How could I help them spend time alone together in an atmosphere that would help them to recapture the spirit of their courting days? I wondered whether they could even remember their courting days, or whether they had even had any courting days. I was certain of one thing: they could not possibly have tied the knot in such a fit of rage.

I took a most unlikely tact with them. I gave them an assignment to get a baby-sitter and go to the Disneyland Hotel and watch the dancing waters. They didn't have to talk to each other or even look at each other. They were to just go there and watch the dancing waters.

The odd thing was that when they came back the following week, they reported, "You don't know what you did for us. We went to the hotel as you told us to do. We walked around and watched the dancing waters. And believe it or not, all of our anger went away!"

I hope that no one reading this will believe that going to visit the dancing waters at Disneyland is a cure-all for all relationship problems. What worked for this couple might not work for another couple. Sometimes in this business, you have to rely on your deepest intuition in dealing with the relationship difficulties of others. My wife and I had gone to watch the dancing waters at the Disneyland Hotel many times, and something in Rick and Diane reminded me of us. I somehow knew they would find the same magic in the waters that we have.

The Philosophy of Play
Sometimes people tell me the reason they don't spend time alone together is that they can't think of anything to do. Sometimes the activities that each partner enjoys are not shared. He likes riding motorcycles, sports, and horror movies. She likes the ballet, gardening, and reading. The only activities they have in common are kids, meals, and chores. When the only things couples have in common are shared responsibilities, fun goes out the window. When he looks at her, all he can see are lawn mowers and diapers. When she looks at him, all she sees are the dirty dishes and dirty laundry.

This is a total disaster. This is the sort of subtle change in a relationship that can cause it to start falling apart. Couples have to learn how to PLAY! Most of us don't even remember how to play by ourselves, let alone in a relationship. Most people have a real problem with the concept of play. They see it as kids' stuff, or childish indulgence.

We are all fascinated by the rich. If this seems unlikely, check out the numerous shows about rich people on television. Why are they so fascinating? The rich know how to play. They have yachts, they go cruising to beautiful places, they play tennis, golf and other sports, and they spend a lot of time in the sun. Hugh Hefner founded the Playboy empire based on the concept of play.

Fortunately, you don't have to be a millionaire to enjoy the benefits of play. It doesn't require a lot of money, and if you really put your mind to it, it doesn't require money at all. But it does require some real imagination, especially if couples have forgotten how to play together.

VARIETY IS THE SPICE
OF LIFE

19

When I do workshops, I have couples make lists of fun things they can do with each other. To help them get started, I encourage them to recall things they did when they were younger, back when they still knew how to play. A few people seem to have no recollection of ever having engaged in anything playful or fun; it is as though they were born totally serious and never deviated from their course. In such cases, I tell them to imagine themselves playing as though they were children. Even the most serious people can eventually get into that.

Some people feel guilty initially about taking the time to be playful, or even about the action itself. Unfortunately, most of us have been conditioned to believe that we need to work hard to make a go of it, and we have also been told that we are acting "silly," "ridiculous," or some other derogatory phrase to describe our playful, childlike actions. When we were little, we were told to get ready to go to school. They when we were in school, we were told to get ready to go to high school. And when we are in high school, we are preparing for college. When we are in college, we are busy preparing for a job. And when we have a job, we are busy preparing for retirement. If all this isn't bad enough, we have people telling us how to prepare for our funerals!

Our whole lives are spent getting ready for something. We have to turn it all around and stop feeling guilty about taking care of ourselves and our mates first. We have to take hold of those 86,400 seconds, quit living in the future, and learn to play and spend time alone with our mates EVERY SINGLE DAY!

The following page offers you a questionnaire to check your skills in paying attention to each other. Take a look at where you are now, honestly and fearlessly. We will talk more in the coming chapters about how to correct each item.

Attention Skills

1.   I look into my mate's eyes for a few moments every day
              Yes   No

2.   I truly listen attentively to what my mate is saying when he or she is talking to me.
              Yes   No

3.   I actively seek out my mate's opinion when I have questions.
              Yes   No

4.   I take my mate into account when I am planning my activities.
              Yes   No

5.   I am sincerely interested in the work or activities my mate is involved in.
              Yes   No

6.   I ask my mate how he or she slept each day, and how he or she feels.
              Yes   No

7.   When my mate is upset about something, I encourage him or her to talk about it with me.
              Yes   No

8.   I really look forward to the time I spend with my mate.
              Yes   No

9.   I think about my mate when I am away from him or her during the day, even on my busiest days.
              Yes   No

10.   I really care about whether my mate is happy or not.
              Yes   No

11.   I plan surprise outings or special occasions to share with my mate.
              Yes   No

12.   At least four times a year, I make time for my mate and I to go away together for the weekend.

                        Yes   No

13.   I am really clear about why I am in my relationship with my mate.

                        Yes   No

14.   My mate is really clear about why he or she is in the relationship with me.

                        Yes   No

15.   If I had to choose all over again, I would still chose my same mate.

                        Yes   No

16.   If my mate had to choose all over again, he or she would still choose me.

                        Yes   No

17.   My mate and I have shared goals and we talk about them frequently.

                        Yes   No

18.   My mate is the most important person in my life.

                        Yes   No

19.   I accept my mate as he or she is, not as I would like him or her to be.

                        Yes   No

20.   My priorities are: relationship first, everything else second.

                        Yes   No

Check Your Score

        Each yes is worth 5 points. If you have 100 points, you can stop reading now. If you have 75 points or more, you are average, and just need a little polishing. If you have 50 up to 75 points, you need to really get busy and put some hard work into your relationship. If you have less than 50 points, you need to get some serious counseling, and it wouldn't hurt to finish reading this book, either!

Remember: Pay attention today or pay alimony tomorrow!

Some Suggestions to Raise Your ATM Quotient (Attention to Mate)

1.   Set aside 15 minutes each day to really give your absolute undivided attention to your mate.

2.   Write a physical description of your mate.

3.   Make a list of all the qualities you really like about your mate.

4.   Make a list of all the areas in your life where you feel your mate is not fulfilling you.

5.   Make a list of all the areas in your life where you feel your mate may not be fulfilling your mate's needs.

6.   After a conversation with your mate, go back over the conversation in your mind or on paper, and see how much of the conversation you actually remember.

7.   Make it a point to tell your mate to sleep well when you go to sleep, and to ask him or her how he or she slept the next morning every single day.

8.   Call your mate during the day and say, "I was just thinking about you, and I wanted to tell you."

9.   Make a list of things you would really love to do. After you have made out your list, mark down the ones that you could share with your mate.

10.   Make a list of the things you have never shared with your mate that you might be willing to try to understand and appreciate with him or her, such as sports, or art.

11.   Plan a mini-surprise for the week to do with your mate. For example, even if you are broke, you could prepare a dinner for just the two of you, get dressed up as though it is a treat out, and even have candles and soft music.

12.   Write a statement of what you are willing to do to make more time to give your mate attention.

Chapter 2

Be Love Finders, Not Fault Finders
A Big Cemetery to bury Partner's Faults: Acceptance

There is so much bad in the best of us and so much good in the worst of us, that it ill behooves any of us to rail at the faults of the rest of us

--author unknown

Bessie, a widow from Michigan had been married for 47 years when as she put it, "My husband suddenly left me to go to heaven." At first she sounded angry about this when I was talking with her at the wedding of her grandchild. We were standing in line for the wedding as part of the wedding procession. "Gosh," she volunteered, "do I miss him!"

I asked her how it was that her marriage lasted for 47 years. "God don't make them any better than him," she told me in a matter-of-fact way. Her very wise statement has stuck with me for many years. I wish everyone was that positive and could accept his or her mate so completely. Her mate could not have received a better eulogy than from this loving person who believed all her life that he was perfect.

Phil, an Italian-American, is an engineer, as well as a rather shy perfectionist and an up-tight, analytical thinker. For thirty-five years he has been married to Wynne, an outgoing Irish-American who says whatever is on her mind. Wynne is a practical, common-sense woman who is relaxed, open and very

25

down-to-earth. The two are opposite in almost everything, yet they have had a fantastic marriage for 35 years.

Why does their marriage work? According to Wynne, "I refused to be submissive to him in his need for perfection and control. We have learned to accept the differences in our personalities and we have learned to become comfortable in sharing our feelings." Differences can enhance rather than destroy a relationship, that is, as long as each person practices acceptance of the other and doesn't try to change or control the other.

As a parish priest for 15 years, I spent many hours with couples in my rectory office helping them with their relationship problems. And for the last 21 years, since my marriage to Shirley, I have spent many hours in my counseling office helping couples with their relationship problems--a total of 36 years. Most of these couples sought my help because their relationships were on the verge of breaking up. One might say that saving relationships is my profession in life. I believe that divorces or breakups often create more problems than they solve. I also believe that a divorce or breakup should be the last of all possible options when there are relationship problems.

The emphasis in this book as well as the emphasis in all my years of working with couples is on making marriages work. Remember, the grass isn't greener on the other side, the grass is greener where it is watered.

Probably the biggest obstacle to making relationships work is fault-finding, which is the opposite of watering the grass. It's an even more powerful destroyer of relationships than trying to control or change your mate. God knows, control issues are behind many a relationship. But fault-finding precedes attempts to control or change. When couples are bickering constantly and involved in destructive fighting, control often becomes the issue as each person attempts to smooth the disturbed relationship again without the proper tools.

Martha and Ann were both married to alcoholics. Martha was filled with hostility and hate toward her husband, while Ann was filled with insight and empathy towards her mate. Martha was hypercritical and righteous, while Ann was tolerant and accepting. Martha and her mate, Roger, had fierce fights that sometimes came to blows. Ann was assertive in a patient, friendly way toward Alfred, her mate, a very negative person who hated his father.

Constantly encouraged by Ann, Alfred got into therapy and joined A.A. Ann spent a great deal of her time working on her own self- improvement. She went to college part-time and joined a theater group. Their marriage survived and got better, and both are now reasonably happy with each other.

Roger got along with everyone except his wife, who was always on his case and had nothing good ever to say to him or about him. Their marriage eventually broke up; today they are both very bitter people.

All Human Beings are Fallible
Marriage is a commitment to love a particular imperfect human being. When counseling couples in my office, it often sounds as though they could write a book about their mate's shortcomings and a page about their own. It is no great discovery that one's mate has a fault, though they always act as if it is. They just didn't see the faults when they were going together, blinded by their unrealistic views of the other person.

Don't Make Mountains Out of Molehills
There are two approaches to marriage: the positive (to see the good in your mate always), and the negative (to do nit-picking and fault finding about your mate). Some people play what I call the "blem game," which is finding some slight blemish in the other's character and blowing it up all out of proportion. In the words of an unknown writer, "There is so much bad in the best of us and so much good in the worst of us, that it ill behooves any of us to rail at the faults of the rest of us."

What is the big deal or discovery about finding a fault in a mate? When couples are first going together, the emphasis is on their mate's good qualities and they downplay the negative qualities. But we all have thousands of traits, most of which are

positive, some of which are negative, and some of which are neutral. There are no monsters or angels in the human race. All of us are flawed.

People come together because they are love finders and not fault finders. Again, I say that the only thing that can destroy a relationship is to do fault-finding. Every human being is limited, we all make mistakes, we all make errors of judgment, we all tend to have things that bug us, we all have shortcomings, we all overreact at times, jump to faulty conclusions, make mountains out of molehills, blow things out of proportion, etc. And, depending on the circumstances, some positive traits can be negative and some negative traits can be positive. For example, being highly critical may qualify you for the job of being a movie critic, but if you are constantly critical of your mate, it will hurt your relationship.

One of the reasons why people fall in love is because they have discovered in the other (at least at that time) that here is a person who accepts them even with their faults, doubts, weaknesses and fears. When two people fall in love they see all the positives in each other. They just can't believe how lucky they are in finding such a perfect mate.

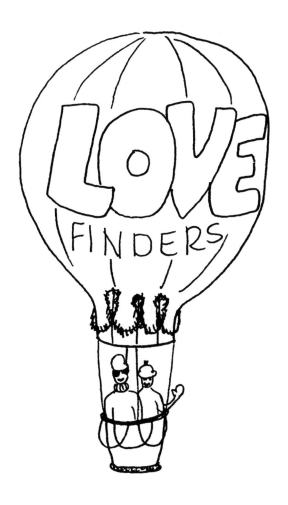

Daniel, on his 50th wedding anniversary, revealed to me that on his wedding day he decided to make a list of ten of his wife's faults which, for the sake of their marriage, he would overlook. Asked to reveal the faults, he said, "I never did get around to writing them down. But whenever my wife did something that made me very mad, I would say to myself, 'Lucky for her, that's one of the ten.'"

Rather than "having a cow," or "going bananas" over the imperfections of your mate, practice acceptance with full knowledge of his or her shortcomings. It is also more fun to try to find things to love than it is to find fault. It is very important to look at our mate in the best positive light.

One way you can very lovingly help your love partner make changes for the better is to encourage him or her positively about the trait you want to see changed. Jess's wife, Sarah, came from a dysfunctional family. One of the results of her background was that she did not really understand very well about taking care of herself physically. Jess was a very clean person, and his wife's lack of personal hygiene bothered him. At the same time, he loved her deeply, so he worked on finding a way to tell her kindly about it. One day he said, "Sarah, I really love you when you shave your legs." Sarah beamed, and from that day on, she made an effort to take care of her personal hygiene regularly.

Very few of the hurts experienced by marriage partners are hurts inflicted intentionally or deliberately. Looking back on a perceived hurt, you or your partner may have made an error of judgement, or may have made an unintentional mistake. Almost all fault-finding results from our distorted subjective interpretations about our mates' behaviors and traits, and from our mental "shoulding" and "oughting" about the perceived shortcomings.

We perceive things about each other inaccurately because of where we are with regard to our own feelings and values. For example, if we have come from a dysfunctional family where there was little love, we may find it difficult to talk openly about our feelings, and a mate could misinterpret that as a fault. Likewise, if you are feeling overtired and your mate wants affection, you could believe that perhaps your mate is oversexed rather than seeing that it is very normal for people who love each other to want to receive affection from each other. And if you chose to overlook the way your mate threw his clothing all over the floor, or the way your mate left the dishes in the sink when you were courting-- things that bother you now--perhaps you need to look at your motives for being in the relationship in the first place.

In reality, we often choose mates who have characteristics and behavioral traits very different from our own. It is often the very things that makes them so attractive to us initially that begin to cause problems later in the relationship. If we really want to make our relationships grow, we can look at those things (rather than at our mate), and what it was about the trait that made it so attractive to us. For example, perhaps one partner is shy and somewhat reserved, while the other is more outgoing.

If someone says to you, "How are you today?" you can answer, "I am fine. I am accepting everyone the way they are." People are the way they are, they are not the way they should be. If you could go your whole day without judging anyone, what a happy and peaceful day that would be.

I am reminded of a Jimmy Stewart movie called "Harvey," the tale of a man who had an invisible rabbit for a friend. All during the movie, the other characters kept finding fault with Jimmy Stewart for introducing his invisible friend. How did Jimmy Stewart handle their criticism? He did not judge it, but instead invited the people over to his aunt's house for dinner. Jimmy remained happy throughout the movie but many of the others around him were unhappy because they were judging instead of enjoying life, people and relationships.

Acceptance Skills Test

1.   I fully accept my mate with all his or her positive and negative traits.

                  Yes   No

2.   I have forgiven everything in my mate's past and do not hold anything against him or her.

                  Yes   No

3.   I am critical of my mate because of financial problems and differences.

                  Yes   No

4.   I recognize that most, if not all, of my misgivings about my partner are related to my own "shoulds," "musts," etc..

                  Yes   No

5.   I am willing to look at my own "stuff" and work on it before I look at anyone else's "stuff."

                  Yes   No

6.   I am afraid that if my mate stays the same as he or she is right now, something terrible will happen to our relationship.

                  Yes   No

. Learn to spend so much time on your own self improvement that you have no time to criticizes your mate. Whenever you feel a need to criticize your mate, remember that the time you spend criticizing your mate could be much better spent working on your own self improvement.

. Learn to praise your mate for his or her faults. Always see that there are two sides to everything. For example, instead of saying that your mate is a cheapskate, say he or she is are a good money manager and give some thought to how you can allocate your financial resources so that everyone can get most of what they need and want. Also realize that your mate may be helping others learn to delay gratification so that in the long run more enjoyment may be had out of life.

. Remember that it is not the events of life that upset us, but rather the point of view that we take of those events.

. Avoid "musterbating!" Get rid of all the "shoulds," "oughts," "musts" and "should nots," "ought nots," and "must nots" about your partner. Musterbating can depress you, and besides that, you could go blind!

. Develop preferences on how you would like things to be rather than demanding that things must be a certain way for you to be happy. In other words, change all your emotional addictions into preferences. Things do not always go the way we want them to. We win some and we lose some. We don't win them all is another way of saying it. So if something doesn't go your way, chalk it up to one of these things that didn't go the way you hoped it might. Or better yet, stop having expectations about everything.

. Really believe that you can eliminate your fault-finding. What we believe, we tend to make into reality. Say the following sentence daily: "I choose my thoughts and feelings, and now, more and more, I choose to find love rather than find fault with my mate."

. Remember that your mate has the right to be the way he or she is. Work on allowing your mate to choose for himself or herself just as you want your mate to do for you.

8.   When you feel yourself starting to do fault-finding try to imagine a big red light going on in your head telling you TO STOP. Immediately count to 10 and tell yourself something good about what just happened.

9.   Love yourself. When you love yourself, you will not burden yourself with the destructive effects that come from finding fault with your mate.

10.   Remember that nothing lasts forever. You can change from day to day, and so can your mate. Just because your mate is depressed or crabby today doesn't mean he or she is always going to be that way. As the saying goes, "This, too, shall pass."

In summary of the above ten points, ALWAYS ACCEPT YOUR MATE WITH FULL KNOWLEDGE OF HIS OR HER SHORTCOMINGS.

BLINDERS ON

How To Make a Marital Lemonade

You can make a game of your mate's alleged shortcomings. Take a look at the following shortcomings, along with the ways you can turn them into positive traits:

Touchy = Very sensitive

Stingy = Very thrifty

Manipulating = Very resourceful

Flighty = Very enthusiastic

Talkative = Very expressive

Rigid = Very well disciplined

Can't say no = Very peace-loving and gentle

Careless = Very easy-going and lenient

Nosy = Very curious, sociable, alert, or aware

Too serious = Very earnest and sincere

Too strict = Very thorough and disciplined

Too bold = Very strong convictions

Too pushy = Very determined, persuasive, or assertive

Too fussy = Likes to do things "first class"

A dreamer = Very imaginative and creative

Overbearing = Very confident

Chapter 3

We All Love Warm Fuzzies Tender Touches Every Day: Affection & Appreciation

A hug is a perfect gift--one size fits all, and nobody minds if you exchange it.
                                        --Ivern Ball

A Thank You Every Day

During every wedding ceremony I perform, I have the couple turn towards each other and say to the other, "Thank you for being my lover, my playmate, my pal, my best friend, my partner, my companion in life."

I tell the couple to do this tomorrow, and the next day. Then I say "Do this all the days of your life together. Look into each other's eyes every day and say thank you for being there." I feel this is one of the best ways of watering the relationship. Both of you try it and see what a difference it will make in your life together.

Friends and Lovers Forever

One of the strange things about doing weddings is pronouncing a couple husband and wife. Before the wedding they were friends and lovers. After the wedding they are husband and wife. Wow, that is serious stuff, this being husband and wife!! But wait a minute!! Are they no longer friends and lovers?

Friends and lovers implies good feelings, playfulness, fun, mutual appreciation and closeness. The words husband and wife are serious words and imply duties, responsibilities and work. It doesn't sound like much fun being husband and wife. It's easy for a husband and wife to forget that they are also friends and lovers.

I have often thought that instead of, or in addition to pronouncing a couple husband and wife, that during the ceremony I should pronounce them friends and lovers forever!! Actually, I am now doing that more and more during the wedding ceremonies I perform.

The Need to Feel Appreciated

Unless we are at the top of the scale in our personal self esteem, we need to hear and receive frequent expressions of appreciation from our lovers. And if we are to water or nuture our relationship, we need to frequently express our appreciation to our partner for being there. Remember, it works both ways. Both have to water the relationship.

To be appreciated means to be valued, to be esteemed, to be recognized and praised for what we do. On the other hand, to be taken for granted (as often happens in a marriage after a while) could lead to the grass not being watered. The relationship can die not because of destructive fighting, but just because it is neglected.

Surprize Your Lover

One of the best ways to avoid neglecting your mate is to use your imagination to surprize your lover with little tokens of appreciation.

Here are some ways to surprize and show appreciation to your mate:

Send a telegram saying "I love you." Leave it unsigned.

Write a love letter. Send it special delivery.

Invite your lover to watch a sunset with you.

Turn back the bed covers on your mate's side of the bed.

Plan a surprize vacation. Make the reservations.

Go away for a weekend on a houseboat.

Make a date for lunch. Take the afternoon off. Go to a motel.

Tender Touching

Skin hunger! The baby cries, you pick it up and it stops crying. We now know in geriatrics that the best medicine for patients is not the technical skills of the doctors or nurses but the bedside manner of those involved with the patient. Babies and elderly long for and hunger for tender touching. But so does everyone else. The need to be touched and hugged to feel good about ourselves and to heal our hurts and wounds is universal.

When I was in the Seminary we were taught that we did not need anyone but God. We were supposed to practice detachment from worldly goods. Human affection was not needed if we were to remain faithful to the priesthood. In the practical world of the Church, there were a lot of conflicts and disappointments. I, for one, needed human understanding. This was especially true when the authorities of the Church punished me for my involvement with civil rights and the farm workers.

A 'PRIEST FACTORY'

Please Touch

At one time, my future wife, Shirley and I were working together, and on her coffee table in her front room was a book entitled *Please Touch*. That title and expression has long remained with me, and over the years I have deepened my appreciation of that expression. Being touched in an affectionate way is very therapeutic and healing.

Affection and appreciation are closely related words. Appreciation is usually associated with something positive done for which a person is thankful, for example, when a mate says thank you for the partner's gift of flowers. Affection is usually associated with tenderness given or received just because of the partner's being. For example, a mate says, "I love you. You are so special to me." Affection brings a couple together and eventually often leads to marriage.

A person needs to continue courting his or her mate all the days of their lives. Each person in a relationship needs to help his or her mate feel special all the days of their lives, not just during the time they are falling in love.

Couples can show warmth or be cold to each other. To be able to give and receive warm feelings is one of the most important qualities a person must have for a successful relationship. This means we have to have a large capacity for affection. To experience coldness can be one of the most painful experiences of life. Unless we have the highest of self esteem, it is one of the most awful feelings in life for our mate to turn cold to us and stay that way for a long time.

The place where we need to start is with ourselves. Learning to accept and to like ourselves and to be warm toward ourselves just for our being is most important. Only as we truly feel warm toward ourselves can we be warm toward others. Affection can be best described as those warm feelings we experience as we love ourselves, as we love another, and as another loves us.

Every relationship needs a lot of T.L.C., i.e. tender, loving care. All three of those words, as simple as they are, form the basis of affection. The most important word in understanding affection is the word "touch." We touch by word, by gesture, by our body language, and by making physical contact. We touch ourselves and we touch others.

To touch in a tender or loving way is sometimes called giving warm fuzzies. To touch in a hurtful way is called giving cold pricklies. A word of praise or compliment is an example of a warm fuzzie.

Touching is not the only way a person can give warm fuzzies or cold pricklies. The best relationships are those in which both partners praise and compliment each other frequently and honestly. The warmest of affection comes when the mind and the heart touch as well as the body.

WARM FUZZIE

COLD PRICKLY

Suppose a lover smiles and says to his mate, "You look beautiful." He gives her a big hug and adds, "I love you." A few moments later he says, "Honey, thanks for picking up my pants from the cleaners." His statements, "You look beautiful" and "I love you," as well as his smile and the big hug, are unconditional strokes that he is giving his mate just for being. She did not have to do anything to earn them. His comment, "Thanks for picking up my trousers," is a conditional stroke that he gives his mate for doing something.

Notice that the above messages are verbal and non-verbal. The smile was non-verbal and the hug was both non-verbal and physical. Some people list physical strokes as the kind they really want. Others like to be told frequently, "I love you." Some mates enjoy the conditional strokes of "Your dinner was magnificent," or "You did a neat job of mowing the lawn."

Once, when I interviewed a couple, the woman responded to my inquiry as to what she liked most about her mate, "He plays with me," she stated in a matter-of-fact manner. She went on to quickly say that she was not thinking of sexual activity but to the kind of play that made her feel good all over because it made her feel so special to him.

Because we are not spirits but human beings with a body as well as a mind and spirit, affection between couples often involves warm tender sexuality and a healthy approach to one's sexuality is very important for the showing of affection.

42

To have a good physical relationship, you need to develop a number of skills. You need to create time to spend with your significant other, not just when you feel like making love, but on a regular basis. Unless you are someone who enjoys making love to a stranger, you need to really spend some quality and fun time with your mate on a regular basis, doing things you mutually enjoy. Even if you have children, you need to find time to be alone. Finding time is probably the most crucial skill you can develop in this fast-paced world.

You also need to develop good communication skills. It is not very satisfying to make love to someone you don't respect and care about, and there are few ways to develop care and respect without communications.

You need to develop some creativity in dealing with your partner on a physical level. One couple was always busy trying to make a living, as most of us are. But the woman took the initiative, and sometimes did totally unexpected things that her mate found stimulating and sensual.

One night when she knew her mate needed a break, she stopped on the way home from work and picked up some good, hot Italian food and a little bottle of red wine. Her husband was upstairs in his office when she got home. She sneaked into the house, loaded some paper plates, napkins, and little wine glasses in the car with the food. Then she went upstairs, greeted her husband, who was lost in mounds of paperwork, and said, "Honey, please come with me. I need for you to go with me right away."

The husband grabbed his jacket and got into the car unquestioningly. She drove the car to a nearby park overlooking the ocean. It was sunset. As she got the picnic things out of the car, her husband smiled and gave her a hug. She knew that if she had asked him to go out to dinner, he would have responded, "But I have too much work to do." But by taking matters into her own hands, and talking to him in a businesslike voice, she was talking in a "language" that he could understand and respond to favorably. As it turned out, they had the most wonderful picnic, watching the sun go down slowly as they ate their food and toasted each other's health and happiness. Do you suppose that they had a loving evening that continued beyond the dinner? You bet they did!

Sometimes it takes a willingness to risk and do something totally off the wall. Sometimes you have to speak to your mate in the "language" of the moment that he or she will understand and respond to. And sometimes you have to take responsibility to create what you really want--what all of us really want--the affection connection!

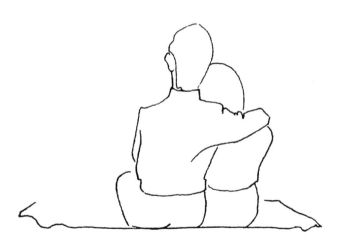

Affection and Appreciation Skills

1. Every day I say thank you to my mate for at least one thing.

Yes   No

2. I take an active part in our sex life and I approach love making with genuine pleasure for both of us.

Yes   No

3. I consider my mate a person of worth and listen with focused attention and eye contact

Yes   No

4. I neither withhold nor demand sex from my partner.

Yes   No

5. I take turns with my mate in initiating sexual love making.

Yes   No

6. Sexually, I am a loving, tender and eager playmate.

Yes   No

7. I have a growing desire for my mate's comfort and happiness.

Yes   No

8. I frequently tell my mate how special he or she is as lover, friend, partner and playmate.

Yes   No

9. I find ways each day to touch and hold my mate.

Yes   No

10. I give my mate at least 3 hugs a day.

Yes   No

11.   I take my spouse for granted and forget to give praise and compliments

12.   I respect my partner's uniqueness as an individual.

13.   I appreciate the many special qualities that my lover brings to our relationship

VALIDATION

Check List of Your Partner's Favorite Strokes

Fill out this inventory of the types of strokes your mate likes.

Receiving a surprise gift ___   Holding hands ___ Going for a walk ___

Dancing ___ Having a conversation ___   Taking a shower together ___

Finding a love note under the pillow ___ Having dinner out ___

Being served a favorite desert ___ Being told "I love you" ___

Being praised for achievements ___   Being approached sexually ___

Doing a surprise chore ___ Being read to ___

Brushing a mate's hair or some other form of gentle grooming ___

Massage ___   Unexpected fun behavior such as chasing your mate ___

What Makes You Feel Most Loved by Me?
What should you do if you really do not know what kind of strokes your mate likes to receive from you.   Try asking the question, "What is it that I do that makes you feel most loved by me?" Your question may take your mate by surprise, but he or she will be pleased that you asked. Also, if you are not getting the strokes that you like the most, take a chance and tell your mate in a friendly way what feels good, what feels fantastic, and what you would like more of.

The Marital Stroke Chart

The chart on the next page has been developed as a simple and fun way to determine how many and what kinds of strokes you give your partner. For one week, each of you can record the number and kinds of strokes you give to each other. Record whether the stroke is positive or negative, verbal or nonverbal, conditional or unconditional.

I think you will find this exercise to be informative and interesting. Also, keeping this record will help you see that giving your mate positive messages requires very little energy. It will help you to eliminate your negative strokes and help you to water the grass where you are. You can make your already good relationship become even better. The more positive strokes that are given and received, the greater the feelings of intimacy and love.

Marital Stroke Card

Positive Strokes
(smiles, hugs, compliments, etc.)

Negative Strokes
(dirty looks, criticism, sarcastic remarks, etc.)

Day 1

Day 2

Day 3

Day 4

Day 5

Day 6

Day 7

LIFE HAPPENS
WHILE WE'RE
MAKING OTHER PLANS

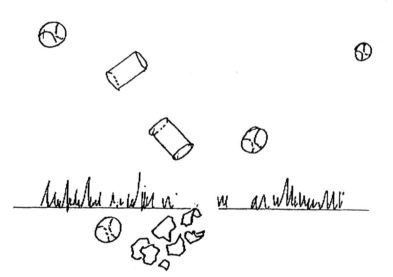

Chapter 4

Life Happens While We are Making Other Plans The Glass Breaks, The Ball Bounces: Adaptability

Alas, how easily things go wrong!
A sigh too much, or a kiss too long,
And there follows a mist and a weeping rain,
And life is never the same again.
-- George MacDonald

If anything can go wrong, it will
--Murphy's Law

Some people say that marriages are made in heaven. But so are thunder and lightning. Of all the areas of life where changes constantly take place, often against our will, there is none more challenging than marriage and family life. Couples evolve through many stages of their relationship and, as children grow up, rapid changes are always taking place. Agony and ecstasy and all places in between are felt in the changing atmosphere of the home.

If Anything Can Go Wrong, It Will--Murphy's Law
Nowhere in human existence is the need for adaptability and flexibility more evident than in marriage and family life. Nowhere is the following expression more true; namely, that life happens while we are making other plans. In fact, THE most important "A" for a successful relationship and marriage is adaptability or what might be better termed "flexibility."

Stepparenting Challenge

I once gave a talk to a group called "Remarrieds Incorporated." My talk was entitled "Remarriage and the Instant Family." Afterwards, a gentleman came up and said to me, "If there are teenagers involved, don't remarry!" While I would not give this advice in all cases, my counseling practice has verified that living with someone else's children poses special challenges to the best of marriages.

Ray was a self-employed Swimming Pool Contractor. He was very orderly, detailed and scheduled. His wife, Barbara, was nurturing, patient, adaptable and tended to avoid conflicts. They were deeply in love. When they married, Barbara had children from a previous marriage. Ray had his ideas on how the children should behave. Also, Ray was severely jealous of the attention Barbara gave her children. He became resentful and cold. Barbara was caught in the middle. She felt like she was in an emotional mine field being the buffer between her daughter and her husband, the stepparent.

Expect the Worst and You Won't Be Disappointed

They came to me for counseling and I directed them to workshops on stepparenting. Together they learned they were not alone in having marital strain over stepparenting. They discovered that their differing expectations were causing them most of their grief. Both learned to accept those things they could not be changed. They came to realize that many of the things they were fighting about were small little things that didn't really matter anyway. Ray grew to the point where he could say, "expect the worst and you won't be disappointed."

The couple is well adjusted now. Instead of an "instant family," they now have a "blended family." According to Barbara, "we blended ourselves to become more well rounded."

Psychologists say that the cornerstones of mental health are high self esteem, effective problem-solving skills and flexibility. There is much attention given to self esteem and, I believe, very little attention given to the most important traits of flexibility and adaptability, or effective problem solving skills. These traits are needed to be able to face and handle the various changes that take place in life and in relationships.

It is important to be able to roll with the punches. A person can either be like a ball that bounces when dropped on cement or like a glass that breaks when dropped on cement. The glass breaks because it is rigid. The ball bounces because it has some give to it, in other words, the ball has some flexibility or is able to adapt when it hits the cement.

Many people grow up leaning toward the extremes of being either a bully or a wimp, a dictator or a doormat, a leader or a follower, a bitch or a "Mr. Nice Guy," aggressive or passive, insensitive or a people pleaser, a master or a servant. We need to learn how to avoid the extremes and how to function somewhere in the middle. In that way we can stand up for ourselves without pushing other people around. We need to learn how to be assertive and appropriately flexible.

BITCH/NICE GUY

MOTHER/SON

MASTER/SERVANT

DADDY/HIS DOLL

Conflict is a natural part of everyday living, whether we live alone or with another person. When two people come together, no matter how much they love each other, their needs, wants, goals and values may clash, creating conflict.

There are positive-positive conflicts, negative-negative conflicts, and positive-negative conflicts. Positive conflicts are choices between two perceived positives. For example, we go out to dinner and the positive conflict is whether we choose steak, lobster, or perhaps none of the above.

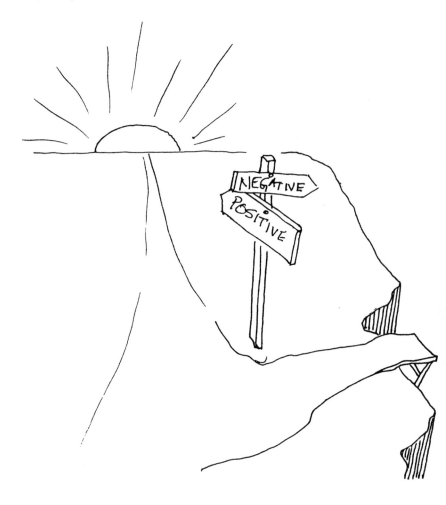

Before he got married, Jack Smith, a plasterer, used to drop by his aunt's house every Christmas eve for a warm family get-together. Since his grandmother passed away many years before, the extended family always went to Aunt Adel's house. There was an unstated expectation that everyone, including new in-laws, would come every year, and tons of guilt were laid on anyone who didn't show. It was an "ultra special." It was more special than "It's a Wonderful Life."

Things began to change for Jack after his marriage to Vicki. She informed him that Christmas Eve had to be spent with her family. He was more than mildly surprised when she informed him that "We'd better be there early. At our family get-together, we don't dare come dragging in late." Not only did she assume that they were going to visit her family, but the agenda also included a tight time schedule. The conflicts that came from both spouses' unstated expectations are obvious.

The Smith's Christmas dilemma is one familiar to all couples, married or living together. Life together as a couple is a series of challenges, problems and conflicts to be solved. From conflicting Christmas schedules, to furniture preferences, to what constitutes a good meal, to when and how the toilet paper is to be changed, to what is great sex, to what is neat and clean, to what constitutes order, to the need to balance the checkbook, to how often to take a shower or brush your teeth are daily conflicts that present themselves even to people living alone. It's just that being a couple seems to emphasize the conflicts to a greater degree.

Family of Origin Expectations

Husbands and wives frequently have different expectations based on their families of origin. They often assume that the way they did things as they grew up is "THE RIGHT WAY," or "THE ONLY WAY."

Rick grew up in a family where it was the custom to eat chicken as well as pork chops with one's hands. Imagine his surprise when he received a less-than-kind note from his mother-in-law through his wife informing him that his manners were considered uncouth.

No Rights or Wrongs in Life

The older I get, the more I realize that there are no rights or wrongs in life, just different ways of doing things. I usually get into trouble when I make this statement, but an exaggeration is needed to make my point. So many adults continue to play the childish game of "I'm right, you're wrong."

Expectations! Your partner's expectations! Your in-law's expectations! Other people's expectations! Oh boy, how they get us into trouble. Expectations are so different about so many things. How can we possibly live up to all of them? And, if the truth be told, we should not. As long as we are following our own agendas and priorities, we should not feel guilty unless we are violating someone's rights. Some expectations, of course, are realistic. For example, you would be justified in expecting your partner to help you when you are ill, or to join in love making when you request or reasonably initiate it.

Other expectations, such as spending an unreasonable amount of time with your parents or in-laws (except under unique circumstances such as critical illness) may be unreal. Expectations change from day to day and we need to be flexible to accommodate all circumstances.

Some expectations are stated, while many remain unstated. It is the unstated expectations or agendas that create misunderstandings as we cannot read other people's minds. Nor should we have to. And many of our own expectations are unconscious until someone else points them out to us. The fact is, we will never have all of our expectations in life met. And that is where compromise comes in. Compromise and sacrifice are pretty much the same thing. Couples who love each other will learn to compromise without feeling as though they are giving up too much.

Realistically, there are flaws in every human connection and we need to learn to accept, in other people and in ourselves, the mingling of the good with the bad. Relationships contain a mixture of blessings and burdens, hopes and disappointments, successes and failures, pleasures and pains, joys and sorrows. I like to say it is a mixed bag similar to the statement, "Work sucks, but I need the bucks."

Couples need to accept this mixture when they promise to be together. As the wedding vows state, relationships are for better and for worse, for richer and for poorer, in laughter and in tears, in sickness and in health, and in good times and in bad.

Most of us, in our hearts, tend to cherish the unrealistic romantic expectations of a vision that "The earth should move and our bones should sing. Fireworks should explode. We should achieve paradise or something almost as great." It is poetic but unrealistic. Some of our greatest moments in life are the smallest things that we scarcely notice in reality.

FIREWORKS OF LOVE

Take a few minutes to think about the things that are really important to you. What are you willing to give up for your relationship, and what do you really need to keep to feel OK about yourself? And what does your mate need? Talk about these things and see if you can get agreement on these items. The test of every relationship is how a couple solves conflicts - do they resolve or perpetuate conflicts?

Adaptability Skills Test

1. I always look for no lose solutions to our conflicts.

2. I believe compromise is the way to solve conflicts.

3. I stick to my principles no matter what.

4. Our decisions are arrived at through consensus.

5. My expectations cause my mate to feel pressured.

6. I resist changes that could add variety and spice to our marriage.

7. I believe that teamwork pays off in marriage.

8. I recognize the role I play in keeping my marriage working and growing.

9. In our marriage, I am part of a caring, loving and winning team.

Couple Conflict Resolution Techniques

1.   Pick the right time and place to resolve conflicts. Don't argue when you are with other people, be it your children, family members, or friends. It could be devastating to children to see their parents argue. It is equally devastating to your partner to argue with him or her in front of other people. No matter how bad you feel at the time, take a deep breath, and think to yourself, "I will handle this later, when my head is clearer."

It also doesn't work to argue when one of you is deeply engrossed in some other activity.   For example, if the man is working on the car, or the woman is in the middle of cooking something.   You could say instead, "I would like to talk with you about something.   When would be a good time?"   Your partner deserves that sort of respect.   If he or she does not deserve respect, what are you doing in the relationship?

2.   Remember to say, "I want to talk with you," instead of "to" you. When you use the word "with," it suggests you are going to try to work on the thing together toward a mutually beneficial solution of the problem.   Talking "to" someone is putting blame on the other person, and putting yourself in a "make-right" position. It infers that you have the problem under control in your mind, and that if your partner would just change, everything would be ok.

3.   Set aside enough time to reach a conclusion to the discussion. It's not a good idea to start something just as one of you is needing to leave the house or to have to take care of some other business. Whatever the issue, it will wait. Also, waiting sometimes allows you to think through the issue more clearly.

Pick appropriate times for dealing with the issue.   Remember all those old comedy routines where the mother greets the father at the door with "Just wait till I tell you what Johnny did today!" Boy, that would really make someone want to come home (to someone else's home).

4.   Be aware of how you are talking during the discussion. Are you using a whiny voice? If you are whining, you are also blaming.

Once you realize how you are coming across, perhaps you can work at being more constructive and less destructive.

5.   Hear what is behind the words being said. "You don't love me," can really mean, "I'm scared and lonely, and I feel as though I am about to be abandoned."

6.   Attack the issue, not the person.

7.   Give "I" messages rather than "You" messages.

8.   Be assertive rather than passive or aggressive.

9.   Try to arrive at a consensus rather than trying to maintain your own way. Remember, there are two people involved. You don't have to "make wrong" to get a consensus.

10.   Deal with present rather than dragging in the past.

11.   Listen openly rather than being defensive. Gather the facts rather than jumping to conclusions. Actively listen rather than interrupting, contradicting, and changing the subject. Try to really hear the issues. And pause before saying anything back. Give the issue a chance to sink in. Sometimes your initial response may be "no," and later change to "yes."

12.   Brainstorm options rather than negating solutions.

13.   See the conflict as we vs. the conflict, not I vs. you.

Chapter 5

Be a Good Ass: Assert, Don't Assume, Don't Attack

Silence propagates itself, and the longer talk has been suspended, the more difficult it is to find anything to say.
-- Samuel Johnson

Jane says, "We can't communicate." Paul replies, "I can't read her mind." Gloria alleges, "He doesn't listen to me." Joe says, "I can't get through to her." Megan says, "He doesn't understand me." And George declares, "We fight, and nothing ever gets resolved."

And so the list of complaints goes on and on. As a marriage counselor, I hear them every day from couples and I wonder sometimes how they have come to this sad state of affairs. More than 36 years ago, when I first began working with couples, all the literature I read and my own experiences led me to the conclusion that <u>lack of communication was the number one problem in marriages</u>. It was by far the greatest difficulty that couples seemed to have in the 1950's. Now, more than 36 years later, I find the same thing to be true. Problems in communication still seem to be the area of greatest challenge for most couples.

Assert, Don't Be Silent or Attack

Going back to childhood, we have all developed a style of getting our needs and wants met. We went back and forth from people-pleasing to attack, from being bullies to being wimps, from being passive to being aggressive, from being dictators to being doormats, and from being leaders to being followers. At a certain point, we decided (generally quite unconsciously) which state of being would be our general mode of operation. We took these stances in lieu of really learning to be assertive which simply means to state what we want in a clear and firm but nonthreatening way. Perhaps it just wasn't safe for us to ask for what we wanted. Or perhaps we never really got a chance to identify what we wanted. But one way or another, the lack of assertiveness has probably broken up more relationships than anything else.

The Effective Communicator

The effective communicator is assertive rather than passive, passive/aggressive, or just plain aggressive. The passive communicator keeps thoughts and feelings inside, assuming the other person knows what he or she is thinking or feeling at any given moment. The passive/aggressive communicator keeps feelings bottled up inside until something causes him or her to explode, dumping all the negative feelings on his or her mate and generally damaging the relationship severely. The aggressive communicator seems to be only able to give messages that come attached to put-downs and make-wrongs. The effective communicator, however, simply states what he or she wants in a clear and nondemanding/nonthreat-ening way.

An Ass Out of You and Me

Mind-reading is one of the biggest mistakes a couple makes in their communications. Human beings are fallible, and it is easy enough to make errors in judgement about what someone says when it is clearly stated. For example, if two people are talking about having dinner out, it is likely that each person will have his or her own idea about what that means. One person may immediately think of a very nice restaurant and dressing up nicely. That person may consider eating out a total experience. The other person, on the other hand, possibly just wants something to eat. Even a quick food place would do in this case. And the person who just wants something to eat certainly wouldn't think of dressing up, or going very far. So you see how easy it can be to misinterpret the unknown.

It's Nice to Know That at Least We Talked It Over

Connie and Terry have been married for 22 years. Connie is a shy perfectionist who works well with children, teenagers, and young adults. She is a school librarian. Her husband Terry is a relaxed, outgoing procrastinator and computer freak. He is employed as a computer programmer.

According to Terry, "We almost never make decisions about our children, expenses, vacations, or bedtime sex without being certain what the other partner wants and trying to agree on what, when and how. When we can't agree, it's nice to know that at least we talked it over."

At First, No Defenses

When I interview couples for their marriage ceremonies and to help them prepare for their married life together, I ask them what they like about each other. Some of the most familiar answers that I hear are "We can talk about anything," "We can spend hours talking to each other," "He is so easy to talk to," and "She listens to me."

Now I know that a lot of those initial feelings are because early in the relationship the couples have dropped their defenses and listen openly to their new-found lovers. They are putting their best foot forward. They are usually most careful in listening very closely to each other. Both are trying to be very cooperative. So what happens? Why the changes? Where does communication break down?

Initially, No Power Struggles

In the early stages of a developing relationship, couples normally do not struggle over who is the boss, over who is in charge, over who is going to call the shots, over who is going to be the head honcho, over who is going to wear the pants in the family, over who is going to make which decision about what. They are not as yet into the dominant versus submissive struggle, the top dog and underdog battle or the bully and the wimp states. The bitch and the nice guy, daddy and his doll, mother and her son, the hawk and the dove, the master and the servant syndromes have not emerged as yet.

Charlie Ara Theory on Couple Power Struggles

I have a theory that every marriage begins with one of the partners more dominant than the other in their style of getting their needs met. And the rest of their lives together, the weaker or more submissive partner is trying to catch up and overtake the other when it comes to power, control, and leadership.

Communication is Social Intercourse

Normally, when we think of intercourse, we think of sexual intercourse, the marriage act, or the culmination of physical love-making between loving partners. That certainly is one way of communication. For lovers, sexual intercourse is a very special way of being close to each other. Because we are human, and not just animals, sexual love-making can have a very deep and special meaning. However, getting into another's mind is intercourse of a social nature. So is getting into another's emotions. We say that communication is intercourse by the spoken word, by letter, by song, by gesture, or by a combination of two or more of these ways.

Definition of Communication

Let me give another definition of communication. Every word of this definition is important. Communication is the attempt to enter into the private world of another human being.

Communication

The word "communication" is taken from the Latin word "communicare" which means "to make known." It is also taken from the Latin word "communia" which means "community." To be united with and have union with another person, as if we are one, is quite a task. In church, we refer to communion, which means to be united with God and each other in a loving way in taking the sacrament of consecrated bread and wine. Communication is an act of sharing. Between partners in marriage, communication might be called a loving act of sharing our inner selves.

Attempt

We use the word "attempt" to signify the effort involved in communication. It is no easy job for two minds to meet no matter how much they love each other. We all have a lot of barriers to receiving and sharing information, opinions and feelings. Our minds may be preoccupied with something else. We may have a deep resentment that prevents us from listening. We may even have a hearing problem, or an active ulcer. Communication is not automatic. We know that businesses spend lots of money on advertising. They study potential customers before they try to get their messages across. One of the basic principles of effective communication is that "what is clear to me is not clear to you." This is one reason why every couple needs to learn the tools of effective communication.

To Enter Into

This means that somehow we have got to enter into the other person's mind through the only avenues that are available; namely, the senses, such as the eyes and ears of the other person. We can joke about ESP. Maybe there is something to it. But I tell couples you have to make very clear and specific what you need and want. Otherwise, it is not fair to blame your partner for not responding to your needs. You have to reach his or her sense of hearing, sense of touch and/or sense of sight. The mind then has to think about what is seen, felt, or heard. Again, communication is not automatic.

Private World

This means that the other person has control over what is going to be let into his or her own private world. All of us have shut-off buttons. We can all be masters of our inner worlds. In psychology, we know that the subconscious of a person has all kinds of armor to prevent penetration of that part of the mind. This brings us to another principle of communication, namely,

that the meaning of the message is in the heart and mind of the receiver.

Of Another Human Being

The other human being is a separate person who interprets the information in the light of his or her previous experiences. That is why it is so important to try to determine where your mate has come from, and where they are presently if you want to communicate effectively.

Self-protection Versus Self-disclosure

To share with another human being implies a certain amount of trust. We have two opposite things going for us at the same time: the need for self-protection and the need for self- disclosure, or what we sometimes call self-revelation. We all have been given a nervous system to protect ourselves from danger. If we perceive a danger from revealing what is on our minds, we tend to be cautious. That is why I say that there is no such thing as love at first sight. We may very much like what we see, but we have to know a person before love can begin. Only as trust and the feeling of safety develop do we tend to disclose who we really are. We tell our significant other about our hopes and dreams in life. We share our values and goals. And when we really feel safe, we will tell the other about our hurts, our dark nights, even our fears, weaknesses and self-doubts. That is when we become genuine to the other, human, with the same doubts and struggles. Now love really happens.

Five Levels of Communication

We talk to each other on five different levels. Each level has its own degree of danger that can be offset only by the degree of safety and trust that is perceived. As we go up the following levels, communication will become more complex and more infinitely challenging.

Level One: Cliche

The first, and safest level of communication, is cliche. This means saying what is expected. For example, "Hello, how are you?" The expected answer is "Fine." You may be feeling lousy, frustrated, depressed, sexy, or fantastic. But you simply answer the greeting with the expected cliche. Suppose you are at the bank and the teller greets you with "How are you today?" You shout your honest feelings back, "I feel fantastic!" The bank teller might misinterpret your exuberance and call the bank manager to deal with you.

FAC

Level Two: Fact

This level is not too risky, but a certain degree of trust might still be needed to feel save when you give an answer. Someone asks you for your name, address, and phone number. The answers are facts, but there might be a certain danger in giving out this information.

OPINION

Level Three: Opinion

The next level of communication is that of opinion. This is where communication starts to become very risky, depending on the relationship. Suppose you are asked about one of the following questions. "How do you feel about legalizing prostitution?" "What is your opinion on abortion?" "How do you feel about women's lib?" "What are your ideas about the death penalty?" "Where do you stand on gay rights?" Our opinions often come from our long-held belief systems and we usually don't like them to be challenged. Since they have to do with our personal values and principles, we can easily get defensive and cut off any dialogue, even with a valued partner.

FEELINGS

Level Four: Feelings

Some people wear their feelings on their faces or in their body language. Most of us, however, are somewhat protective of the feelings going on inside of us. The healthy person knows how to express feelings in ways that are appropriate in terms of time, place, and circumstances. Very private people keep their feelings well hidden and tend to be brooders. Keeping negative feelings suppressed too long may lead to deep distress, causing premature heart attacks, strokes, and other psychosomatic illnesses. In my experience, brooders tend to be alcoholics and go from being passive to being aggressive.

TOTAL HONESTY

Level Five: Total Honesty

I often hear, "I want my mate to just be honest with me." This may seem like a reasonable wish, but marriage counselors have developed some reservations about total honesty. Does our lover need to know every detail about our past life? Is the need for total honesty really based on communication needs, or is it based on the false need for security and control? Is the need for total honesty a cover-up for one person's hidden agenda to control the other? At what point can a person share all and know that he or she will be accepted totally unconditionally. I would venture to say that not even two saints could do that!

The Almost Saints

Mickey and Al were model parishioners. They held classes in religion in their home: the classes were geared for teenagers. In their own words, they have been married 46 short years and had raised seven boys and one girl. They were active not only in their church, but each had a career as well.

On one occasion they shared with me that they both had short tempers due to a communication misunderstanding. They had agreed to meet at a certain intersection at 5 P.M. and go to dinner. Al related, "I was at the corner five minutes early, and I waited for an hour. At first I was concerned about Mickey, and then I got really steamed. I finally decided to go to another corner of the same intersection. You guessed it, Mickey was on the other corner, equally steamed. It was a terribly busy and large intersection, and neither of us could see across the street. Just think! A little more detail on which of the four corners of the intersection they were to meet would have avoided the misunderstanding.

THE MEETING AT A STREETCORNER

The Effective Listener

There are many principles to effective communication. One of them is to be an effective listener. Some of the qualities of effective listening are to look at the person, value what the person has to say, ask questions for clarification, remain neutral rather than defensive, and learn to give good feedback. For example, if someone makes a statement that doesn't make sense to you, repeat it back to them, saying "What I am hearing you say is ... ."

Sensitive, effective, objective, and complete listening is a difficult tool to develop as we all tend to jump to conclusions before we get all the facts. This often happens because we have developed mind sets, and closed minds about certain topics or situations that we have previously experienced. That is why we all need to practice the art of having an open mind, and to try to get all the facts and information before we make an opinionated statement or judgement. Better yet would be to have insight as to where the speaker is at the moment. In this way you can hear behind the words and understand what the other person really means.

Some Guidelines for Positive Communication With Your Lover

1.   Use lots of "I" messages such as "I feel," or "I think."

2.   Make your communication positive. Assume you can improve your relationship and work forward from that point.

3.   Avoid unfair communication techniques (mind-reading, switching the subject, interruption, contradicting, silence, etc.

4.   Be clear and specific.

5.   Test all your assumptions verbally rather than second-guessing.

6.   Invite your partner to explain whatever is unclear to you.

7.   Accept all feelings and try to understand them.

8.   Attack the issue and problem, not the personality (disagree agreeably).

9.   Make yourself totally attentive to your partner when he or she is talking.

10.   Be open and accept without judgement the feelings of your partner.

11.   Learn to when to use humor and when to be serious.

12.   Be kind, tactful, considerate, and courteous.

13.   Don't yell, whine, or nag.

14.   Avoid turning discussions into destructive arguments.

15.   Remember that each event can be seen from different points of view.

16.   Give feedback on what you have heard.

17. Ask questions for clarification.

18. Value what your partner has to say.

19. Be a sensitive and effective listener.

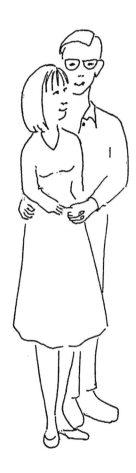

HEALTH/VIGOR

Chapter 6

Accentuate the Positive Wonderize, Don't Horribilize: A Zest for Life Animation

No two human beings have ever made, or will ever make, exactly the same journey in life.

--Sir Arthur Keith

Now I am Alive

For awhile it was our secret; Shirley and I were to be married. If it became public knowledge, I would have to leave my parish church assignment. A Roman Catholic priest was not supposed to fall in love and get married. Slowly, I began to tell a few trusted relatives and close friends, among them, Mark, a Maryknoll missionary and brother of Corita Kent, a famous artist. I wasn't certain what his response would be as he and I had been close friends over the years. It was with mixed emotions that I told him.

A few days later, Shirley and I received a colorful banner with the following inscription, "I was dead. Then you came, now I am alive." Later, Mark pointed out how alive I seemed to him when I was telling him of my love for Shirley and the excitement of the new beginning that was in store for the two of us.

Mark made a good point. Of course we weren't really physically dead, but our love made us appear so much more alive. We would have many obstacles to overcome right from the beginning, challenges such as finding employment. Imagine that!

We were both unemployed when we got married. although we didn't know what the future would hold for us, our spirits were high. we were optimistic about our future despite the many problems we would have to face.

We have now made it for more than twenty-one years. We have experienced the hopes and disappointments, the joys and sorrows, the pleasures and pains, the successes as well as the failures of married life.

What has helped us greatly has been our positive approach to the many challenges of life together.

Get All the Help You Can

Scott and Jill, married 28 years, are two very open persons. Both are ranchers. Scott is an attorney. Jill spends her time working on church, community and charitable activities. Their two children recently graduated from college.

What has made their marriage work? According to Scott, both have a strong desire to make a good marriage better. As a consequence, they use every tool available to them. For example, they have attended a Marriage Encounter which was a positive experience for them. They have "date night" and "family home activities."

They are familiar with all the Biblical passages that speak to a good marriage. Jill referred to the one where the Lord tells them "do not let the sun go down on your wrath." They often pray over the passage in I Peter 3:8 "In summary, keep your love for one another at full strength." They also mentioned seeking professional help in counseling when needed to search out what was best for their spouse and children.

Accentuate the Positive

Back in the 1940's I remember learning and singing a song that I always liked. It has stuck in my heart for these many years. I don't remember the title, but the words went something like this, "You got to accentuate the positive, eliminate the negative, and don't mess with Mr. In-between." Practicing the A's of Affability,

Amiability, and being Animated have helped us accentuate the positive.

The Two People in each of us

Andrew Carnegie, author of the Power of Positive Thinking, felt that everyone had a dual personality. One personality was negative and the other personality was positive. How well one functioned in life depended on which personality a person decided to use in his life.

Being Positive Made It Work

Recently, I ran into an old friend by the name of George, a serious minded scholar type, who had been married for 20 years. He and his wife had some tough times with business losses, a developmentally disabled child among their five children, career disappointments and personal illness such as diabetes.

I asked George what one thing kept them together over the years and he said "the Lord." I said, "Come now, George, that's not the answer I want. If you are on a lake or ocean and a storm comes up, yes, you have to pray to God but you also have to row toward shore. God can't do it without you. Besides the Lord, what other one thing finds you still married to the same person today?"

George thought about it for a while and finally said, "I must give my wife the credit. It was because of her enthusiasm that we are together today." George went on to explain how his wife was such a positive, lively and zestful person. Even when they were down and out and saw their life savings go down the drain in a business venture, his wife remained positive and brainstormed alternatives of what could be done.

Now that's a great example that we can all learn from because there are a lot of setbacks in life. And it is having a positive attitude about the negative times that can make the difference.

So What!!! Now What!!!

I have always advocated that when disappointments happen in life to say SO WHAT followed by NOW WHAT. Life is a serious of challenges with every day having a number of problems to solve. Couples who have a zest for life and are positive in their thinking can enjoy the many challenges and problems of life. To put it into church terms, we all need to have the virtue of hope. Hope is the opposite of despair.

Be a Person of Hope

This world of ours is filled with many prophets of gloom and doom. But a couple who practice both affability and amiability will be animated with a positive approach to life and will make their marriage exciting and alive. So what are the characteristics of a person of hope or of a hopeful person?

I see three qualities as making up the optimistic or upbeat person. First, the person actively uses alternative thinking and doing. Second, the person is a collaborator, and third, the person has a true zest for life.

The Alternative Thinker and Doer

Jane asked her friend Frances where she had gone on her past vacation. Frances replied, "San Diego."

"Where did you go the previous summer?" Jane asked.

"San Diego," Frances stated, matter-of-factly. "We always go to San Diego." How boring!

Variety is the Spice of Life

Some people live 365 days a year. However, many people live the same day 365 times. It is more exciting to have a change once in a while rather than do the same thing over and over the same way. Some couples always go to the same restaurant or always order the same food.

I once knew a man who for forty-five years only drank Scotch on the rocks. How dull. Just think of all the unique tastes he had missed, not that I am promoting heavy drinking. But there is so much more out there.

To keep a relationship alive, both parties need to use their imaginations to face their many challenges. In a sense, there are no problems in life. There are only challenges, possibilities, choices, alternatives, options and different paths.

A BORING MARRIAGE

For example, instead of having sex every Saturday night at 8:30 p.m. with fifteen minutes for foreplay and one minute for orgasm, a couple could take some initiative and try some different times, places, and even positions. Remember, it takes two imaginative people to keep a relationship exciting.

Be a Collaborator

If anything is going to make a loving relationship work it is teamwork. Perhaps the word collaboration is somewhat foreign in our everyday language. It really means to co-labor and to work together. Some people are better at working together than others. But loving relationships take teamwork. In a marriage, when two are pulling together as a team, it is a sign of real hope that the couple can accomplish together the many tasks that come their way.

If we live long enough and get involved in joint ventures with others, sooner or later we may get burned. A business deal with a partner may fail and the partner blames us or we blame the partner. That is the risk we take by being involved. When people get burned in a business venture, they may vow never again to form a business partnership. But join hands, we must, especially if we are to have loving relationships. Just because we have been burned once does not mean we have to be on the burner for the rest of our lives!

A team approach works best for couples who want to make it. They can look at themselves as coworkers, cohabitants, and cooperative partners. Oh, there might be some struggle as to who is the captain of the team. But a couple could work out who does what best and have that person take the lead in that specific area. But both people need to be on the same team, not on opposite sides.

Someone observed that the Bible states in the Book of Genesis that "the two shall become one." That set off a big argument. Which one? With open discussions and compromises on both parts, both parties can win and get their individual needs and wants met.

A Person of Zest

Finally, the person of hope is a person of zest. Call it aliveness, call it enthusiasm, call it spunk. Nothing of importance was ever accomplished without enthusiasm. When two people fall in love (or fall in lust), they are very alive to each other and have a lot of time and energy for each other.

Keeping up the positive energy is the task of both partners. However, nothing takes away energy faster than negative emotions. Anger, depression, guilt, anxiety, and distress are the great enemies of animation, affability and zest.

When we think and feel positive, the juices of motivation flow in the body and we have enormous energy to accomplish whatever needs to be done. On the contrary when we think and feel negative (stinkin' thinkin'), all our energy seems to go away real fast.

People who are always tired out, are people who quickly use up all their energy in their negative thinking. Depressed people usually are not interested in sexually loving their mate because they have used up all their energy feeing bad. Gosh! We have better things to do with our time than to spend our time feeling bad!

Both partners in a relationship should get into the habit every morning of going outside and saying, "Hi world, this is a great day. I feel happy, I feel healthy, I feel great." Whenever I start my day this way, it fills me with a lot of energy for the whole day.

When asked how I am, I try to always answer, "I'm alive, well, everything works, nothing hurts." Or I say, "I am great, I am accepting everyone the way they are." I try to always be positive.

83

Affirmations & Positive Attitudes

My spouse and I are on the same team.

My spouse and I are in alignment.

I use my own brains and any other brains I can borrow.

I am an alternative thinker and doer.

I join hands with my partner.

I am a person of hope.

I am a person of zest and energy.

I put on my PMA (Positive Mental Attitude) every morning

I focus on the good and positive in my mate

I look for the good even in the worst of situations

Steps In Creative Problem Solving for Couples to Practice

1. Try to get a full picture of the problem.

Why is the situation unsatisfactory? What is the background and history of the problem? Are there two or more sides to the problem? What are the needs or objectives that are not being met? Why do different people see the problem in different ways?

2. Try to brainstorm several solutions without judging them

What might be done about the problem? What options and choices are available? What are possible solutions? What might work or be tried?

3. Evaluate each of the solutions proposed in step 2.

What are the advantages and disadvantages of each solution? Is there a solution in which everyone wins? What are the risks involved in each solution? What information do I have?

4. Try to come up with the best decision after evaluating.

What is the best of the alternatives? What feels right? What will minimize risks?

5. Implement the decision by definite action.

When will it be done? How will it be done?

6. Follow up the evaluation.

Did the decision and action solve the problem? How did it work out? What would I do different next time?

Chapter 7

Agreeability: Get a Sense of Humor: Affability, Amiability

To Look at the Sunnyside of Everything and Make Your Optimism Come True
                              --Optimist Creed

Gardners for Fifty Years

Jack & Mary have been married for over 50 years. I have known them for 36 of those years. They were one of the first couples I met after my ordination. They were passionately involved in both the intellectual and spiritual life of the parish to which I was assigned. I keep in touch with them to this day and respect their opinions about the church and family life.

Not only is Mary a literal gardener, she sees her marriage as a garden that has always been well watered. First of all, she says that she and Jack were "well prepared soil." Before they were married both their fathers had left their families forcing them to learn responsibility early in life. At the time, both had similar religious values, as well as similar financial backgrounds. Looking back on it, their expectations and temperments were also similar.

Mary recalls on their 25th aniversary, Jack said, "My motivation has always been to please you." And Mary said, "that's odd, because I think I am doing everything to please you!" WOW! That's a lot of watering! Not a bad idea, to try to please each other. "Besides," Jack recalls, "We have given each other a lot of space to do our own thing, which gives a feeling of freedom within a close relationship."

So You Don't Have Any Problems

When I am interviewing couples in preparation for their upcoming marriages, I usually ask them how they handle conflict. Sometimes they tell me, "Oh, we don't have any problems. We agree on everything." I chuckle to myself because I know that the only people who do not have problems are people in cemeteries.

Exact Opposites

I remember a dramatic moment in a family counseling session. The oldest son was asked by the therapist how he saw the family. Without a moment's hesitation, he blurted out, "Mom and dad are exact opposites." Well, what else is new? No two human beings are exactly alike.

In many ways, we are all very different from each other. The old joke was that the man was the "head" and the woman was the "heart." Although the old joke was also the opposite; namely, the woman really wore the pants in the family, only her man did not know it. With all joking aside, no two human beings are exactly alike. In fact, the more we look at each individual, the more we realize how unique each person is. In the words of one of the Marriage Encounter songs, "There is no other you."

Two Unique Miracles of the Universe

Your mate is a unique miracle of the universe. Wow! Notice the word "unique" and the word "miracle." No matter how much lovers have in common and no matter how much they like each other, each partner in a relationship is still a separate human being. As such, each partner has years of experience in interpreting his or her own world. No two human beings feel exactly the same about everything in life. Each has his or her own opinions, values, and ideas. This is perhaps why couples fight about the three most fun things in life, namely sex, money, and kids.

No two people have exactly the same set of priorities, and in a relationship there is going to be constant need for negotiation and compromise. So what happens when you put two unique miracles of the universe together in a marriage? There are bound to be disagreements. Needs will clash. Some values will clash. Opinions will conflict at times. Wants will clash. Goals will clash. Priorities will not always be the same. There will be lots of conflicts.

Two Yuppies

It was a marriage of three years. Mark and Tricia were a young couple trying to get ahead. Were these yuppies sitting in my office on the verge of divorce? It was the mid 1980's. Both had children from a previous marriage and now they had one of their own. They were two strong bright individuals.

Mark was very controlling and aggressive. Tricia was outgoing and spontaneous. At first, Mark entered therapy by himself. He had been feeling a lot of guilt over leaving his first wife for Tricia with whom he was now in fierce frequent arguments. Many of their arguments were over their ex spouses and how visitation of the children was to be handled.

Fantastic Sex or a Living Hell?

Mark was seriously considering returning to his first wife. Besides wanting to handle his guilt, Mark saw this as a way to spend more time with his children from the first marriage. Tricia was infuriated. Theirs had become a love hate relationship. Fantastic sex but the rest of the time a "living hell."

After hearing their stories, my first words to them were, "The grass isn't greener on the other side, the grass is greener where it is watered." The couple agreed to look at their destructive patterns and learned to give up the kind of love that was restricting, conditional and demanding. We had many painful therapy sessions, some individual, some together but always intense.

Mark continued to struggle with his decision to return to his first wife. But somewhere in the course of therapy he decided that his marriage to Tricia was the one "to water." So he began to "water the grass" with Tricia. It is now five years later and the couple reported to me that the counseling really helped them. Their marriage is working well and they are glad they stayed together. Both say that they water the grass every day especially by listening to each other.

Problems Are Challenges

That's why it is important to look on problems as challenges and opportunities to grow. Actually, it could be quite exciting (given positive attitudes) for a couple to face their challenges together. It is much easier to do that if they are affable and amiable.

How Two Devout Lutherans Did It

They had been married 25 years when they came to see me for counseling. They were devout Lutherans very involved in their own local church. Their presenting problem and major conflict was their two difficult teenage adopted boys, John, an aeronautical engineer and very controlling, described their kids as "two very physical, non-academic jocks growing up with nerd parents."

Toni, a very warm, supportive-type person, was an emotional doormat frequently caught in the middle. She was loyal to her husband but would protect the boys from the wrath of her husband.

At first, the parents had high expectations for their sons, and had great difficulty coming to terms with their limited abilities versus their expectations. They saw their boys as having "instant gratification" and "cause-effect" problems.

The therapy was difficult. John and Toni had different approaches to parenting. This was putting a strain on the marriage. The couple had to decide what was most important; namely, maintaining their affection for each other or forcing these boys to become what they were unable to become.

Fortunately for them, John and Toni decided to ride out the teen age years and concentrate on their love and support for each other. Another example of a couple "Watering the Grass" and saving their marriage.

As Toni put it, "we both tried to support each other. When one of us was going bonkers, the other tried to be rational. We made a real effort to keep the garbage from undermining the real affection we hold for each other."

What's in the Marriage Contract?

Marriage is complicated by the fact that it is the only contract that people make in which they do not agree to anything except vague generalities. Unless there is a prenuptial legal contract, the only thing a couple really agree to (at least in the State of California) is to divide their property equally in the case of divorce.

Would you go to work for a company for a vague salary? Would a company hire you with only a vague understanding of what your job and hours would be? Just suppose you went to work for a company because you liked them and they liked you. It would never work out just on that basis. Or if it did work out, it would be a short-lived professional relationship.

Life Through the Looking Glass

I believe all hurt is the result of some faulty perception, some incorrect interpretation that we take personally. Instead of just allowing the person his or her opinions, we feel threatened and take on a "fight or flight" stance.

But is it any wonder that we have that sort of response programmed into us? Look at the way we grow up. We are born with total self esteem and total self acceptance. When a child is born, everyone normally loves it. Cute baby, sweet baby, pretty baby are some of the first words we hear. Then we start to walk, and we fall down, and we keep trying to get back up again. Everyone cheers us when we finally make it. No one says, "Stupid kid can't walk right."

But then with walking comes our curiosity and exploratory nature, and the message changes. "Get away from that stove. You'll hurt yourself." "No, stop that." "Don't touch that lamp!" And suddenly we become aware that we have limitations and that we're not quite okay. And we come to see the world as a dangerous place where we will get hurt at every turn.

When we are being potty trained and we make a mistake, we get even more messages to let us know that we are inadequate. Now the message is even stronger; things that are as natural as breathing are areas where we can mess up!

Then we go to school and we encounter the grading system. We are judged by the number of items we get wrong, never applauded by the number of items we get right.

And when we develop careers, the ulcers and heart attacks begin to happen as we repeatedly try to please the seemingly unpleasable. We may receive our rewards and accolades for a job well-done, but there is always the nagging message at the back of our minds that "one screw-up and we're out the door."

We are judged negatively by our society in almost all aspects of our lives. Even in church, we hear that we are sinners. What about the song, Amazing Grace? Amazing Grace/How sweet thou art/That saved a wretch like me. . . Even the most beautiful songs declare that we are wretches, imperfect wretches. What a dismal thought!

None of us want to feel inadequate, yet at every turn we encounter personal "make-wrongs." Somewhere along the line we all need to be totally accepted by someone other than ourselves. Hopefully, that person can be your mate.

Two Keys for Healthy Relationships

Self esteem and appropriate flexibility are two keys to healthy relationships. If you're feeling good about yourself, you're not going to lay that trip on your mate to always make you feel good.

I have heard many people I've counseled tell me, "My mate drives me crazy." I hate to disappoint you, but that's not true. We drive ourselves crazy when we try to control the outcome of everything in our lives.

We have to give up trying to be the manager of the universe. We will be healthier mentally when we realize that the most control we can have is to realize that we have no control. There are no guarantees in life.

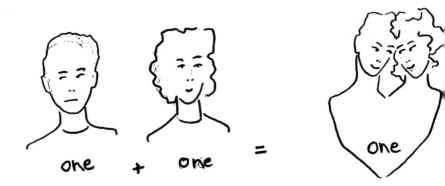

94

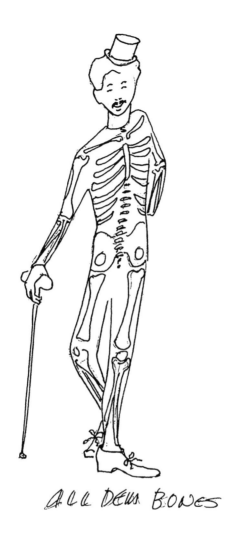

ALL DEM BONES

All Dem Bones

To have a good marriage, good mental and emotional health, you have to have a backbone, a funny bone, a crazy bone, and a wishbone. You've got to have a sense of humor. Humor comes with appropriate flexibility. Learn to roll with the punches. Even the dark side of life has its humorous aspects.

Getting Rid of the "Grungies"

There's nothing that upsets us or drains our energy more than anger, except guilt, anxiety, or depression. Those four negative emotions are sneaks, cheats and liars. We need to stop renting out our heads to those negative emotions; we have better things to do with our time than to feel bad.

BANDAGED
HEART

"Grungies" are hurts that we carry in our systems. The grungies are like having a javelin with a two-edged sword on it. They are what happens when you try to get revenge on the person who hurt you. It ends up hurting you more in the long-run. Get rid of the grungies. What does it matter anyway? The past is dead; it's over. The past is dead, the future is unborn, and there's only now, and now is okay.

Mr. Fixit, A Sports Nut and House-Husband

Jim and Ann have been married for 44 years. Jim is retired and takes care of the home while Ann works for the Gas Department. Both enjoy gardening and do that together. Ann jokingly says her husband would live on the golf course if baseball weren't invented. The stress of taking care of elderly parents has brought them closer together. What made their marriage work according to Ann? She says "Couples need to get away from one another once in a while - otherwise you'll suffocate each other and getting on each other's nerves can cause big problems."

How to Grow a Funny Bone

1.	Rent a funny movie or watch an old, funny movie on TV at least once a week with your mate.

2.	Leave funny notes and cartoons hidden all over the house where your mate will find them.

3.	Go to the park with your mate and play basketball, frisbie, baseball, or fly a kite.

4.	Save little humorous stories from the newspaper or magazines and read them to your mate at the breakfast table.

5.	Put on some old dance music and play Fred Astaire and Ginger Rogers with your mate.

6.	Have "foot fights" in bed. Put the bottoms of your feet up against your mate's and push as hard as you can. A pillow fight can be truly fun too.

7.	Put a "smiley face" on your mate's breakfast toast.

8.	Learn to do creative hugging: right knee of your mate clasped between your two knees, left knee, both knees between your knees, right elbow between your elbows, left elbow, etc.

9.	Play like children. Chase your mate around the breakfast table. Buy a train set and play with it. Lie on the rug and color pictures together with crayolas. We have lost our ability to see through a child's eyes.

10.	Go to fun places together regularly. Miniature golf is always fun. Or go to a carnival, a county fair, or a 		water slide. Ride in bumper cars at Disneyland.

11.	Keep a "should" diaper handy where you can both find it. The next time either of you uses the word "should," run and get the diaper and say, "Oh, oh, I just should on myself!"

12.	Remember that the things going on in the outside world are "outside." You can still be happy about your own private world. You don't have to dismalize. If the news is making you sad, think about doing one positive thing that you can do to help make a change and do it.

13.	Do volunteer work. There is nothing to help develop a caring and loving sense of life than helping others to feel better.

Chapter 8

The Biggest Room
in the World:
Your Lover Has a
Right to Grow:
Affirmation, Allowance,
and Approval

The privilege of a human being is to change.
                              -- Jeanne Moreau

". . . I will love you and help you to become all that you wish to
be." These words are taken from the vows and wedding promises I
have every couple say to each other during the wedding ceremony.

Can I Be Married and Still Be Me?
Richard was 15 years older than JoAnne when, as he said,
they "fell in lust." Initially they were both fun loving, spontaneous
and open to life. Because of their differences in age, Richard had
to resist the temptation to parent JoAnne. As the relationhip
progressed, Richard began to suffocate her and his possessiveness
became obsessive. This intensified when Richard had a spiritual
experience and became a religious zealot.

Richard tried to change JoAnne's behavior to conform to what
he believed was right. However, JoAnne was at a different place in
her life and needed space. For a short time, she left the
relationship to make a life of her own. Richard loved his wife very
much. He prayed and learned to love her unconditionally. He also
learned to stop being judgemental of her. This was hard for him as
his controlling nature wanted to lecture, change and make

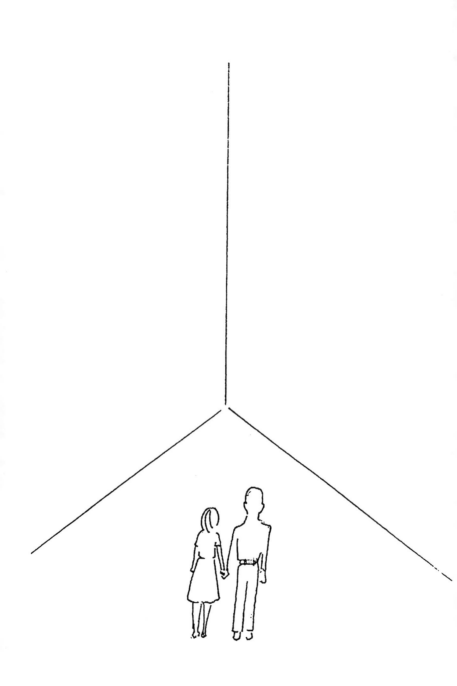

decisions for her. He came to the point where he was able to let go of her and was able to give her the freedom to make her own choices.

Their communication opened up and JoAnne told Richard that God hadn't moved her the way Richard was moved by God. Richard resisted the temptation to say "I hope God knocks you on your . . ."

A short time later they experienced a 6.0 earthquake. Richard got out of bed, went to his wife's apartment and brought her home. Both had changed outlooks. Today they are both much more comfortable in their relationship. Richard has given up controlling and JoAnne can be married and still be herself.

Does Your Mate Need Your Permission?

I had quite a struggle to find the right word beginning with A to describe the emotional support a person needs from their mate in order to become the person they wish to be. Some people suggested the word allowance. I did not like that word because it seemed to imply that you needed your mate's permission to change and grow.

A lot of people make the mistake of trying to control their mate and are very threatened by any positive changes their partner may try to make.

The focus in this chapter is on affirming, assisting, allowing and approving the right of your lover to grow and become the person they were meant to be.

Say Yes to Your Lover

I like the word affirmation. It is my favorite word to describe emotional support. To affirm means to say "yes."

Giving emotional support to your partner's growth and activities is an essential in nurturing a relationship.

Beyond emotional support, helping to make things happen for one's mate is the way to affirm. Actions speak louder than words.

Affirming is supporting the right of your partner to be different, their right to be a unique individual, the right to have his or her own values, opinions, and ideas, etc. even when they are different from yours. To affirm means to give space to your partner to be his or her own person.. A healthy relationship balances togetherness and individuality.

How good it feels when your mate affirms your plans to become a better person. How good it feels when they support your efforts to grow and change for the better. When you both give each other mutual support, the relationship is at its best. On the otherhand, how stressful the relationship becomes when you or your mate tries to control and keep the other where they are at. It seems that in these days of changing roles in relationships, that men are more often guilty than women in preventing the other to grow.

Women's Liberation

Want to start an argument? Ask the question, "What do you think of women's lib? Despite my male chauvinistic upbringing, I have been a supporter of women's liberation for many years. I guess this goes back to my days of being for the underdog, for the civil rights of minorities, the rights of the farmworkers, the rights of the poor, the elderly and the layperson in the church.

It seems I have joined every liberation movement since then: the sexual revolution, children's rights, gay rights, and I have opposed the lust of power wherever I saw it.

More Barefoot than Pregnant

I bring all this up because in my work with couples, I have found that the role of women outside the home continues to be confusing. Consequently, many men are very fearful and threatened when their mates want to grow, have a career, and generally want a role other than being barefoot and pregnant.

A marriage can reach a period of great strain when a non-assertive type woman begins to grow, assert herself and develop a career. Some men still feel they own and possess their woman. Thus they try to control them. I am amazed at how many women tell me in therapy that they have to get their husband's permission to do this and that. I thought all that went out the door in the 60's. However, I must say that sometimes I find the opposite true today in the 90's. There are many aggressive women who dominate and control their mates who have become sensitive and caring guys.

Single and Celibate

In my days as a parish priest, I used to stand in the pulpit, single and celibate, and tell people how to be married and how to raise their kids. At that time I was not married and did not have any children. I lived in a rectory; do you know what a rectory is? A rectory is a home for unwed fathers.

A 'PRIEST FACTORY'

Now that I am married and have five children, I realize how little I knew about both marriage and raising a family. In fact, before I was married I had five theories on how to raise children. Now that I have kids, I gave up on all those theories.

Life has all types of changes and interesting twists in it.

None of Us are Done Yet

None of us are done yet. As I have said before, "The biggest room in the world is the room for improvement." We can all always improve our interpersonal skills, our money management skills, our problem solving skills, our communication skills, our eating habit skills, and our love-makng skills. Improving is a lifetime task that goes on twenty-four hours a day. For some people, it might even feel like more than that. I like to say that is why it is so important to spend so much time on your own self-improvement that you have no time to criticize your mate.

Say Yes to Your Mate

Again to repeat, to affirm means to say "yes." Giving emotional support to your mate's growth and activities is an essential in nurturing your relationship. Beyond emotional support, helping things happen for your mate's growth and activities is a way of affirming life. You are supporting the right of your mate to be different, to be a unique individual with his or her own values, opinions, ideas and dreams. In doing so, you are ultimately improving the quality of your own life. In otherwords, you are saying "Yes!" to your own life.

Eulogize, Don't Categorize

In 1971, I was giving a talk at a Unitarian Church when a woman came up to me and declared in an angry voice, "You men." I stopped her and said, "Wait a minute. I am not "you men.' I am Charlie, a unique miracle of the universe." Needless to say, my answer stopped her and made her understand that she was perhaps guilty of "categorizing" people.

Perhaps our changing roles in society have made us all more or less guilty of being less than accepting of others. Perhaps the shaky foundations we stand on create the need to feel that it is too scarey to allow others to be who they are. Women are afraid that if their men talk to other women, or God forbid, have friendships with them, that ultimately they will lose their men to the other women. And men suffer from the same fears. And there is the feeling that if the other person does whatever he or she wants to do, perhaps what he or she will want to do is close the door on the relationship.

A SAFE HARBOR

A Safe Harbor

Bill, a salesman for many years in the carpet business, called for a counseling session. I had seen him about ten years before when his previous relationship had broken up. Shortly after that, I had performed his wedding ceremony to his new bride, Maureen, a very positive, upbeat person. As far as I knew, their marriage was great, so I wondered what the problem could be.

Sad to say, I learned that Bill had contracted cancer a year after they had married. However, his cancer did not interfere with their marriage and their desire for a good life. Maureen was most supportive of Bill as he searched for the best methods of treating his cancer. He admitted that a positive thinking program helped the most in arresting his cancer. He and Maureen remained best friends and lovers for the remaining eight years of his life. Then the cancer spread and he passed on.

I was asked to give the eulogy and I talked to Maureen privately about Bill before doing so. She said that her years with Bill were the best of her life. "We never stopped nurturing each other. Our life together was always an adventure. We were always affectionate, supportive and appreciative of each other. Bill gave me a safe harbor where I could splash, grow, and flourish."

The Grocer and the Housewife

Louie and Dory have been married 42 years, and have 7 married children and 18 grandchildren. Both are superachievers and having a large family in no way prevented them from reaching their individual goals. Louie started out as a box boy at a grocery chain and now owns his own chain of ten supermarkets. He has been president of the California Grocers Association. Dory describes him as a perfectionist who is always on time, always efficient, and who takes lots of pride in his work. Dory sees herself as outgoing and diplomatic. She considers very few things in life worth fighting about, especially children and money. Dory has been a champion golfer and tennis player who has played at most of the famous courses in the world.

When asked about what made their marriage work, Dory replied, "You have to make your spouse think he is wonderful and the best. Tell him how lucky you are. It pays lots of dividends. You have to support your spouse. Ninety-nine percent of the time, loyalty is most important. Enjoy the simple things in life, no matter how much you have or want."

Balancing Space and Togetherness

Kahlil Gibran begins his commentary on marriage by saying "You were born together and together you shall be forever more.

Chapter 9

B.O. and S.O. (Body Odor and Soul Odor): Keep Yourself Appealing and Attractive

If you can't be a golden pippin, don't turn crabapple.
--Pieties quilt, collection of the
Museum of American Folk Art

Happy People Make Happy Marriages

We have all heard the expression, "Happiness is an inside job." It is a myth to believe that your partner is supposed to make you happy. You and you alone have the power to make you happy. Never give it away to another human being. When a person is happy, and does not need someone else to make himself or herself happy, and feels he or she can each maintain their own happiness and have something to contribute to the other person, then that person is ready for a healthy relationship. For example, a couple could be talking about their sex life together and the one would say, "You've made me so happy because of the way you have physically and emotionally loved me." And the other person would say, "That came about because you are such a happy and loving person."

But let there be space in your togetherness and let the winds of the heavens dance between you."

Tom, a retired plumbing contractor, was an extreme perfectionist which made him somewhat uptight. His wife, Joyce, was also a perfectionist but to a lesser degree than Tom. In addition, she was very outgoing and light hearted which helped relax Tom. It was the second marriage for both. They have been married for 16 very happy years. Both had felt smothered in their previous relationships.

From the beginning, both encouraged the other to have fun activities with friends of the same sex. Tom liked to play pool and he often had his friends to the house. Both were into golf and Joyce often had her lady golf friends to the house. So, besides having friends together, they also had their separate friends. According to Joyce, the young today call this giving your mate "space," but she calls it "just common sense."

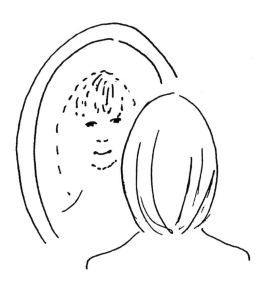

An Appealing Compliment

John, an autoworker from Detroit, was married to Joan, a giver type and super responsible type woman. Her style was to do for others and play the victim and martyr. John was a functional alcoholic who got along with everyone except his wife who hated his drinking. She would give him vicious tongue lashings every time he came home under the influence. While John insisted that he could go without drinking, he often went to the bar after work rather than come home to a bitching wife. She was the all time master of the "cold prickle." The couple had not made love in over a year. The couple were sticking it out in a rotten marriage because of their deep love for their remaining son who was a teenager.

As the marriage counselor, it was hard for me to tell if he drank to get away from her or if she bitched at him because he drank. The marriage was on the verge of breaking up when he came to see me. The reason for their coming was to deal with their grief at the death of their 24 year old son who had been killed in an auto accident. The hostility between the two of them had temporarily been put on hold because of the family tragedy. I suggested that the two of them stop trying to change the other and to start giving each other at least one compliment a day starting right there in my office. With great reluctance, John told her she was a great cook. With even greater reluctance, Joan thanked him for fixing the kitchen sink. For the next several sessions, we reviewed the compliments each gave the other and the couple decided they would stay together. They even started having intercourse again. Amazing what a complement can do!!!!

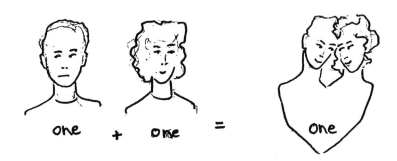

one + one = one

Positive Qualities are Appealing

It takes 74 muscles to frown and 24 to smile. How easy it is to turn a frown upside down!!!! Each person in a relationship can develop his or her own sense of humor. The ability to see the funny side of things is a very attractive quality. Smiles spread themselves and cost nothing.

Communicate in an Appealing Way

Neither the bully nor the wimp are attractive. The bully sends his message with a missile. The object is to attack. The mate receiving this kind of message tends to get defensive and withdrawn. The wimp doesn't speak up but his or her mate gets the message that something is wrong. The body language of the wimp becomes stressed, sad and unattractive. Often the wimp goes from being passive to aggressive and finally blows up at his or her mate, pushing them away. When a person says what is on his or her mind in a friendly way, that is appealing.

Turn- Offs Damage the Relationship

The following list of behaviors and attitudes that smell bad was developed in a class I had on relationships. Those attending wrote down what their mates did or could do to damage the relationship. Read the list. Check the ones you do sometimes. If you are doing any of them, I bet you can stop. After all, you don't want to smell bad emotionally.

_Hold grudges _Use abusive language _Does not say he cares

_Not interested in my activities or growth _Drinks excessively

_Takes me for granted _Fails to follow through on promises

_Criticizes me in public _Attacks my values and goals

_Not wanting to see my side of the story _Nags me

_Tries to control the relationship _Embarrasses me

_Does not take time to listen to my dumb little problems

_ Compares me with past lovers _ Interprets situations in a negative fashion _ talks excessively about his or her ex-mate

_Is inconsiderate of my expressed needs _shuts off communication with me _Walks away with a frown

_Fingerpointing _Assigning blame when things don't work well

_Puts too much restrictions and limitations on my behavior

_Acts bored and disinterested in my comments about what occurred at work _"Chip away" at my ego to enhance his own

_Acts as if the relationship is not very important to her or him

_Not showering or brushing teeth before coming to bed _talks down to me like a child _Being demanding

_Does not allow me to be myself _Bring work tensions and worries home _Puts friends and career before me

_Does not acknowledge the child and the needs of the child in me

Behaviors That Smell Good

The following list of behaviors and attitudes that smell good was developed by the same group of couples that came up with the ones that smelled bad. Each partner listed what his or her mate did that he or she liked and that was appealing. Check the list for the ones that you can do to make your relationship smell better.

_Dresses up for me _Accepts me fully as a person _ We play a lot _Gives encouragement as I work _Plans surprize dates

_Makes me feel important _Helps me conquer my weight problem

_Spends more time together _Compliments me, especially around other people _Sends me "I miss you cards" _Is a good listener _Has a sense of humor _Laughs with me

_Being supportive of each other's careers _Being less critical _Try to accept my mistakes as mistakes

_Uses gentle techniques of persuasion _Enjoys my personality

_Offers advice only when asked _Helps me to have confidence in myself _Assists in decisions about raising children

_Helps me through stressful situations _Verbalized appreciation of me _Tries new things with an open mind _Is generous with time and money _Shares his ideas _Is first and foremost my best friend

113

Affirmations for Appeal

I keep myself in shape so that my mate is not repulsed by m appearance

I keep myself in excellant shape both mentally and physicall both for my partner and for myself

I shower and/or bathe every day

I brush my teeth every day

I keep myself in a positive mood for myself and my partner

I have a positive sexual self image

I catch myself when I am in a crabby or bitchy mood

I no longer dump my negative moods on my partner, or oth members of my family

I wear my PMA (positive mental attitude) around the house

Appeal is an interesting word. When we are attracted to drawn to someone because of the pleasurable qualities of his her mind, spirit, emotions, or body, we call it appeal. The way person dresses, walks, or talks is directly related to his or her se image. We all recognize consciously or unconsciously whe someone has a positive physical self-image.

Appeal also has to do with the mental and spiritual ways person approaches life. A complainer is hardly appealing anyone, nor is a person who is constantly putting others dow The people we most often perceive as being attractive are thos people who make us feel good about ourselves, and those wh have something worthwhile to offer in life.

A person who sees God as a loving spirit, rather than one wh is always punishing is appealing to us. A person who radiates sense of humor and happiness about life, even when things aren always going well, is the person we remember as being a beautif person, an appealing person. The person who retains a sense of personal dignity and respect for others has a great deal of personal appeal for all of us. Such a person is someone we remember all our lives.

What would it take for each of us to become appealing people? If we remain appealing by taking good care of ourselves physically, mentally, and spiritually, our mates, as well as other people, will want to be around us. Being attractive to our mates requires the greatest attention to our own mental, physical, and spiritual needs and wants. We cannot give to others what we cannot give to ourselves.

ANGEL OUTSIDE
DEVIL AT HOME

The Bad Odor of Negative Moods

Many people are devils in their own homes and angels in the world outside. "Stinkin' thinkin'" Joseph, a successful salesman, knows how to woo people in the marketplace. He is also an expert at handling rejection, and keeps up his positive mental attitude when he is dealing with clients. At home, however, his attitude stinks. He transfers his negative repressed emotions from the market place to his home. He spends most of his hours at home being sullen and angry, and allowing himself to become irritable over the smallest things. His wife and children often walk on eggshells to avoid his nasty moods, staying away from home whenever possible.

The sad thing is that the place that could be a sanctuary for the whole family is nothing more than a garbage heap where everyone is covering up anger and hurt feelings.

Martha, a hairdresser, listens kindly to her clients, putting up with their gossip, their coming in late, and their sometimes unreasonable demands. She seems to have it all together. Yet when she comes home, she frequently engages in "B.E.L.T.," Bitching about Everything in Life Today. It reminds me of the bumper sticker that says 51% lover, 49% bitch.

Without tending our personal gardens properly, we can quickly become 90% bitch and 10% lover or even worse. No one would consciously choose to live in a home where such negativity prevails. Yet many people live in such environments until they become so miserable that they take some drastic action, hurting each other seriously, or leaving the situation altogether.

Two Approaches to Life

As it is with everything in life, there are two approaches to looking at things, positively and negatively. Everything has a positive and negative side. Look at eating. Eating is necessary to stay alive, but if you don't eat the right food, not enough food, or too much food, you will suffer physically and mentally. Even oxygen, the one thing we can't live without for very long, can do harm to us if we get too much of it.

There are many stresses facing all of us today outside and inside our relationships. But how we face those stresses is key to our well-being. We can remain appealing in life and handle everything that comes our way if we always remember that we are ok, no matter what else happens. We can deal with it.

Don't let your relationship begin to grow weeds by allowing yourself to become unattractive emotionally, mentally, and physically. If you are thinking right now, "Life is really bad," ask yourself, "As compared to what???" If you are feeling bad when you get up in the morning, turn it off, look at your mate, and say, "Boy, I feel really challenged today!" Or how about asking your mate for help or support in your efforts? We have been raised up to believe we always have to go it on our own, and that is really "stinkin' thinkin'."

There is nothing wrong with asking for help, support, or even a hug when we begin to feel bad. Allowing ourselves to be vulnerable is probably one of the most appealing qualities we can possess as human beings. And it makes our mates realize how important they are in our lives, rather than cutting ourselves off from them and leaving them stranded out there, feeling alone and wondering what they ever saw in us.

Whether you feel stressed out or really positive, stop, take a deep breath, and tell yourself, the next moment is a brand new start. Sit down together and eat nutritious meals every day, even if you must rush somewhat. Try to get up earlier and take a little walk, meditate, or get some exercise. And you don't have to do it all alone either. If your mate is overweight, say, "Let's eat better together. We'll feel better and look better, and I really want to support you in being the beautiful, healthy person I know you are."

Take a few minutes each day to find something positive to read to each other. It can be a funny article in the newspaper, a cartoon, or even a good saying from a book of quotations. There are many such books available on the market today. Make it a goal to find something good each day to report to your mate.

Make it a rule to go to bed at a reasonable hour. If you or your mate (or both of you) are out of sorts, talk it out before going to sleep. And make certain that you get quality sleep, and as much sleep as you can reasonably manage. You will not feel on top of things if you wake up tired and have been grinding your teeth all night. And it will hardly make you an attractive person.

Wake up each morning and be thankful for being alive and having all your faculties. Be thankful for having an opportunity to make a brand new start. And be thankful for having a mate who loves you by your side.

It's All How You Look at It

Mary and JoAnne each had workaholic husbands. Mary, on the one hand, played the P.L.O.M. game (poor little old me), and presented herself as a depressed, angry, and victimized woman, hardly attractive qualities for anyone. She spent many lost hours trying to change her husband's behavior, all to no avail. JoAnne, on the other hand, took her opportunities in hand and enrolled in college, taking courses for self-improvement. Spending her time on her own self-improvement, her husband began taking an interest in her new interests, and eventually began to spend a little more time with her.

When you feel attractive mentally, physically, and spiritually, others perceive you that way and things will go better in every endeavor. As you believe, so shall it be. If you perceive yourself to be rich, you are rich. If you perceive yourself to be poor and unattractive, so it is. We have all known someone in our lifetimes who was in reality poor, yet seemed somehow wealthy. And we have likewise known people who seemingly had everything money could achieve, and yet led really impoverished lives spiritually and mentally.

We See What We Want to See

We are besieged on a daily basis by bad news of one kind or another, in the newspapers, on the radio, on television, and from the mouths of others. We can choose to see the bad side of everything, or we can try to see if perhaps there isn't another way of looking at a situation. Yes, many people are out of work, and there are numerous social problems. How can we be positive and attractive when we deal with such realities of life?

It is all in the way we look at things. I am reminded of the concentration camps of Germany. They had to represent man's darkest side. Yet there are records of drawings left by children who were in the camps--drawings of flowers and butterflies and beautiful things. How could children in such a situation possibly come up with such beautiful images? Surely they suffered the same physical, mental, and spiritual depravities as the adults. And yet, they drew flowers.

There is never only one way to see anything in life. Look at the cactus. There is beauty even in that which has thorns. Life is full of hills and valleys waiting to be traversed. The road will never be straight; it will meander through the hills and valleys, sometimes turning back on itself, sometimes making us think we are lost. But we are never lost if we have a destination. We are never unattractive if we look up instead of down.

Personal Ecology

We all take an interest in the world's ecology; it is one of the hottest topics of the century. We realize how important it is to keep a balance on the earth if we are to have an earth in the future. We must also realize how important it is to practice personal ecology. Your body, mind, and spirit represents your personal universe. Take care of it and practice ecology of your precious world. You will be rewarded with a sense of the beautiful person you really are.

Appeal Skills Checkup

1. I frequently find myself in a rotten mood.
                    Yes   No

2. I never seem to have enough time to do anything I want to do.
                    Yes   No

3. I fall asleep with problems on my mind more than I used to.
                    Yes   No

4. I sometimes wonder whether I am physically or sexually attractive to my mate.
                    Yes   No

5. The more I see of the outside world, the more negative I become.
                    Yes   No

6. If my mate would just change the way he or she does certain things, I feel that I could be a more attractive person.
                    Yes   No

7. I feel attractive but . . . (answer yes or no if this thought has ever occurred to you).
                    Yes   No

8. I'm not sure being an attractive person will make any difference in the way people treat me.
                    Yes   No

9. I will be attractive when . . . (answer yes or no if this thought has ever occurred to you).
                    Yes   No

A.S.K. (Appeal Skills Knowledge)

1. Take good care of your body, staying clean, eating properly, and getting sufficient rest and exercise.

2. If you are in a profession where you are surrounded by negativity, make it a point to do some positive activity each day (read a good book, attend motivational lectures, attend church, and make and cultivate friends who are highly positive.

3. Look at yourself carefully and objectively in the mirror each day. Have someone make a video tape of you while you are talking. Are you coming across in a positive, appealing way, or do you need a brush-up or touch-up?

4. Do you take good care of your clothes, making sure they are cleaned and pressed neatly? Do you try to wear the nicest looking clothes you can afford? Even if you don't have a lot of money, you can buy nice clothes at a thrift shop. If no one has ever said you look nice in your clothes, get a friend to help you pick out some different clothes. Sometimes we simply don't know how to dress in ways that are becoming to us.

5. Work on setting goals each week, both alone and with your mate. It is easy to set goals for yourself and forget about having any with your mate. Check each other on your progress in working toward your goals every week.

6. Make it a point to say something good about your mate and one other person every single day.

7. Make it a point to think and/or say something good about yourself every single day.

Chapter 10

Commitments for the 21st Century: Two Together Can Make It Work

After a while you learn
The subtle difference between
holding a hand
and chaining a soul
and you learn
that love doesn't mean
leaning
and company doesn't always mean
security.
And you begin to learn
That kisses aren't contracts and
presents aren't promises ...

--Veronica Shoffstall

In the days before it was acceptable to live together before the marriage ceremony, I used to joke and say that "getting married was like taking out a learner's permit." I studied 12 years before I could perform the duties of a priest. A Registered Nurse is four years in training before practicing nursing. The same is true for many other professions in life.

Marriage is no easy task. There will be so much to learn along the way. Yet to get married no legal preparation is required beyond taking a blood test and getting a license. Even a teenager has to take out a learner's permit before getting a driver's license.

Tools for Your Relationship Tool Box

What is the future of relationships as we approach the 21st century? Well, pairing up is certaily here to stay in some form or another. So for you involved in a couple relationship or about to be involved in a long term relationship, you will want to have all the tools you can to make it work.

Nine Signs That You Have the Tools for a Successful Relationship

You and your mate both have or are working toward the following:

1)   A large capacity for affection

2)   Emotional maturity

3)   The capacity to communicate effectively and appealingly each other's thoughts and feelings.

4)   A zest for life

5)   The capacity to handle tensions constructively

6)   A playful approach ot sexual love making

7)   The capacity to accept fully the other person with full knowledge of his or her shortcomings

8)   Realistic expectations

9)   Both to have high self esteem and appropriate flexibility

These nine signs of a successful relationship have been explained in the various chapters of this book. It is my hope and prayer that your relationship with the lover you have chosen will bring you fulfillment and may you have, in the words of my opening prayer at a wedding, "a meaningful, successful, fulfilling, exciting, playful, stimulating, challenging, growing and happy married life together."

Sometime ago I remember reading a survey of men and women on what they thought made their marriage work and what kept their relationship going. Most of their answers had to do with their positive attitudes and beliefs about their partner. Men and women answered slightly differently but agreed on their top seven responses in the order of importance. They gave about 15 responses and reasons which I want to share with you. The kinds of things which I remember they said were the following:

1)   I consider my spouse to be my best friend

2)   I very much like my spouse as a person

3)   I believe marriage is a long term commitment

4)   Marriage is sacred

5)   We agree on aims and goals

6)   My spouse has grown more interesting

7)   I want the relationship to succeed

8)   We laugh together

9)   We agree on how and how often to show affection

10) We discuss things calmly

11) We agree on a philosophy of life

12) I confide in my spouse

13) We agree about our sex life

14) We share outside hobbies and interests

15) I am proud of my spouse's achievements

16) We have a stimulating exchange of ideas

Learning is what life is all about. It is not the destination, it is the journey that counts. If you knew that right now would be the last moment you would spend with your mate on this earth, how would you live this moment? What would you want to say to your mate?

Perhaps the simplest things in life are truly the riches that life has to offer us. Wealth comes and goes in our lives. Cars break down. Houses need repainting. Even children grow up and are gone in a moment. But a moment well-lived with a mate can last a lifetime.

When you look at your mate, remember what it was about her or him that made you fall in love in the first place. If things aren't right with the relationship, make them right.

Time, the Delightful Thief

Time, the delightful thief
Steals from all, without relief.
Whether we be great or small,
Time has no respect at all.
Where songbirds sang in the sun today,
Tomorrow snow falls and children play.
And not a trace of the crime is shown,
Except for a world that has so grown.
And still shall come another day
That time, the delightful thief
Shall steal away.
-- Anne Copeland MacCallum

We insure our favorite possessions against loss. We take all sorts of precautions to protect our valuables. Yet the true valuables in life, our best friends and lovers, we often overlook. How could you insure against the loss of your mate? I don't mean it in a monetary sense, but in the sense of having to replace that person. Could you ever really replace that person.

No matter how many times you may have been married or have lived with another person, each person you have encountered along your life's path has enhanced and enriched your life in some way. And you have enhanced and enriched the life of the other.

There is little in this world that cannot be changed or fixed, short of death, and scientists are working on that one. We live, in some ways, in the most fortunate time. There have never been more self-help books, support groups, encounter groups, types of mental and physical therapy available to help you make it as a couple. Anyone who says "We can't" in this verdant jungle of relationship improvement tools is really saying "We don't want to..." Someone once told me that her mother told her that there was no such word in the English dictionary as "can't."

Perhaps part of how we change and grow in our relationships has to do with how we talk mentally to ourselves. As I said earlier, we can either be a horribilizer or a wonderizer. Which will you choose to be?

If your mate is really beyond help, say goodbye graciously and lovingly and move on. Why would you stay with something that has no hope of working right? Is your own soul so impoverished that you cannot allow yourself someone better? But beware of how you see the need to find someone better? Prettier? Richer? More fun? More intelligent? Thinner? More sexy? I am willing to bet (and I am not a betting man) that you will simply encounter more of the same. When you look at your mate's faults, if you believe your mate has faults, think about how you might change to see them differently. As I said earlier, and will repeat, Look into your significant other's eyes every day and thank him or her for being there. Think about watering the grass. The grass is really greener where it's watered.

A Dozen Ways To Get Time Alone — For Lovers

1. Have set times when the TV will be turned off.
    TURN OFF THE TV!!!!!!

2. Take the phone off the hook when you have set time aside to be alone.

3. Make dates at least a month in advance and write them down on your mutual calendars.

4. At least once a week, have a weekday or a Saturday morning breakfast out at a restaurant.

5. Take an evening walk once a week enjoying the evening air and holding hands.

6. Get away to a hotel or motel once a month for 2 nights and 3 days.

7. Find a juccuzzi to sit in late at night.

8. Take a long auto drive getting out of the car every few miles to take a short walk together.

9. Go to the beach or park in the early evening to watch the sunset.

10. Exercise together in the morning.

11. Establish firm family rules for the children, e.g. from 9 pm is mommie's and daddie's time alone. You have had your time with them.

12. Have a good strong lock for your bedroom door.

13. Etc. _____
    _____